THE PASSAGE OF DOMINION

R. William leckie, jr

the passage of dominion: geoffrey of monmouth and the periodization of insular history in the twelfth century

UNIVERSITY OF TORONTO PRESS
Toronto Buffalo London

© University of Toronto Press 1981
Toronto Buffalo London
Printed in Canada

ISBN 0-8020-5495-1

Canadian Cataloguing in Publication Data

Leckie, R. William, 1940-
  The passage of Dominion

  Bibliography
  Includes index.
  ISBN 0-8020-5495-1

  1. Geoffrey of Monmouth, Bp of St. Asaph, 1100?-1154.
  Historia regum Britanniae. 2. Great Britain – History –
  To 1485 – Historiography. I. Title.
  DA129.5.L42   942.03   c80-094740-1

FOR NIKI

CONTENTS

pReface

The present study examines one aspect of Geoffrey of Monmouth's reception in the twelfth century, namely the impact of the *Historia regum Britanniae* on notions regarding the periodization of Insular history. Following the appearance of Geoffrey's imaginative depiction, writers engaged in a variety of endeavours found it necessary to grapple with a new and very pressing problem: At what point could dominion be said to have passed from the Britons to the Anglo-Saxons? The difficulties posed by this question make themselves felt not only in compendious surveys, but also in Latin recensions and vernacular paraphrases of the *Historia* itself. Although the number of examples in any given category is relatively small, taken together these texts provide a clear line through the twelfth century, one which reveals a great deal about changing attitudes toward the Galfridian version of events.

The necessity of dealing with such a wide range of works has imposed certain limits on the investigation. The textual footing is seldom as secure as one might wish, and many of the vexed questions surrounding the manuscript transmission of individual texts lie outside both my competence and the scope of the study. I have involved myself in the discussion of the relative chronology for the three principal recensions of the *Historia regum Britanniae*, because here the handling of the periodization would seem to have important implications. For all other works I have relied on the available scholarship, mindful that the current state of knowledge varies considerably from text to text.

Interest in at least some of the relevant works runs high, and there is cause for optimism regarding the prospects for significant advances. New editions of the *Historia Brittonum* (David N. Dumville) and of Henry of Huntingdon's *Historia Anglorum* (Antonia Gransden) can be expected in the foreseeable future. As progress continues to be made, specific points in my discussion may well be found in need of modification, correction, or elaboration. I offer the x Preface

present study as a framework within which certain aspects of Geoffrey's reception can be better explained. My hope is that it will both prove useful and will spark additional work in the area.

It has not been practicable to provide complete bibliographies for all the works and subjects touched upon. Wherever pertinent, I have cited the most recent studies, and here the concerned reader will find fuller listings, especially of earlier scholarship. In preparing the notes I have used a system of abbreviations and short-titles throughout. Complete references can be found in the final list of Works Cited.

A number of people have read and criticized this study at various stages in its preparation. My colleagues Angus Cameron, A.G. Rigg, and Michael M. Sheehan graciously took time out from their own work to give me the benefit of fresh perspectives. Their detailed, thoughtful comments brought about many changes, and I can only hope that they approve of the final result. In addition, three anonymous readers went over the penultimate version for the University of Toronto Press and the Canadian Federation for the Humanities. The names of these individuals are not known to me, but I wish to thank them for their painstaking and very helpful reviews. I have had excellent advice, and what errors remain, whether factual or judgmental, are mine alone.

Major portions of this investigation first took shape during several summers spent in lush subtropical surroundings at the University of Miami, Coral Gables, Florida. I should like to express my appreciation to Paul G. Feehan and the staff of the Otto G. Richter Library for the many courtesies extended to me over the years. Special thanks are also due to University of Toronto Press and particularly to Prudence Tracy who guided both the manuscript and its author through the editorial process with patient good humour. This book has been published with the help of a grant from the Canadian Federation for the Humanities, using funds provided by the Social Sciences and Humanities Research Council of Canada, and a grant from the Andrew W. Mellon Foundation to the University of Toronto Press. Without such generous subvention my scholarly labours could not have appeared in their present form.

The book is dedicated to my wife Niki, who has an aversion to the kind of sentimentality often found in statements of gratitude. Let it simply be noted that she provided what I needed most to bring this project to completion: a lot of patience, timely nagging, and flawless typing – not necessarily in that order.

Mississauga, Ontario
January 1980

ABBREVIATIONS

AB Alfred of Beverley *Annales, sive Historia de gestis regum Britanniae* ed
Thomas Hearne (Oxford 1716)

ÆC Æthelweard *Chronicon* ed A. Campbell Nelson's Medieval Texts (Edinburgh 1962)

ASC *The Anglo-Saxon Chronicle: A Revised Translation* ed Dorothy
Whitelock with David C. Douglas and Susie I. Tucker (London 1961)

DBG C. Julius Caesar *De bello Gallico* ed Otto Seel *Commentarii rerum
gestarum* 1 (Leipzig 1961)

DEB Gildas *De excidio et conquestu Britanniae* ed Theodor Mommsen MGH:AA,
13 (Berlin 1898) 25–85

EdE Geffrei Gaimar *L'Estoire des Engleis* ed Alexander Bell Anglo-Norman
Texts, 14–16 (Oxford 1960)

Faral Edmond Faral *La légende arthurienne* 3 vols Bibliothèque de l'École des
Hautes Études, Sciences historiques et philologiques, 255–7 (Paris 1929)

FV First Variant *Geoffrey of Monmouth, Historia regum Britanniae: A
Variant Version* ed Jacob Hammer Publications of the Mediaeval Academy of
America, 57 (Cambridge Mass. 1951)

GC Gervase of Canterbury *The Historical Works* ed William Stubbs 2 vols Rolls
Series (London 1879–80)

GRA William of Malmesbury *Gesta regum Anglorum* ed William Stubbs 2 vols
Rolls Series (London 1887–9)

Gransden Antonia Gransden *Historical Writing in England c 550 to c 1307*
(London 1974)

Griscom Geoffrey of Monmouth *Historia regum Britanniae* ed Acton Griscom
(London, New York, and Toronto 1929)

HA Henry of Huntingdon *Historia Anglorum* ed Thomas Arnold Rolls Series
(London 1879)

HAP Paulus Orosius *Historiarum adversum paganos libri* VII ed C. Zangemeister CSEL, 5 (1882; repr Hildesheim 1967)

HB *Historia Brittonum* ed Theodor Mommsen MGH:AA, 13 (Berlin 1898) 111–222

HE Bede *Ecclesiastical History of the English People* ed Bertram Colgrave and R.A.B. Mynors Oxford Medieval Texts (Oxford 1969)

HRA William of Newburgh *Historia rerum Anglicarum* ed Richard Howlett 2 vols *Chronicles of the Reigns of Stephen, Henry* II. *and Richard* I., 1–2 Rolls Series (London 1884–5)

HRB Geoffrey of Monmouth *Historia regum Britanniae* Faral, 3: 64–303

LB Layamon *Brut* ed G.L. Brook and R.F. Leslie 2 vols EETS, 250, 277 (Oxford 1963–78)

O'Sullivan Thomas D. O'Sullivan *The 'De excidio' of Gildas: Its Authenticity and Date* Columbia Studies in the Classical Tradition, 7 (Leiden 1978)

Partner Nancy F. Partner *Serious Entertainments: The Writing of History in Twelfth-Century England* (Chicago and London 1977)

RD Ralph Diceto *The Historical Works* ed William Stubbs 2 vols Rolls Series (London 1876)

RdB Wace *Le Roman de Brut* ed Ivor Arnold 2 vols SATF (Paris 1938–40)

RT Robert of Torigni *Chronique* ed Léopold Delisle 2 vols (Rouen 1872–3)

RW Roger of Wendover *Chronica, sive Flores historiarum* ed H.O. Coxe 4 vols (London 1841–2)

SG Sigebert of Gembloux *Chronographia* ed L.C. Bethmann MGH:SS, 6 (1844; repr Leipzig 1925) 268–374

Tatlock J.S.P. Tatlock *The Legendary History of Britain: Geoffrey of Monmouth's 'Historia regum Britanniae' and Its Early Vernacular Versions* (Berkeley and Los Angeles 1950)

THE PASSAGE OF DOMINION

THE PASSAGE OF DOMINION

iNTRODUCTiON

From standard authority, popular tradition, and his own fertile imagination Geoffrey of Monmouth fashioned a rich, if tumultuous, history for the Britons. The *Historia regum Britanniae* chronicles the deeds of a flawed people, in whom the potential for greatness was matched and often surpassed by the capacity for folly. The achievements of brilliant commanders and sagacious rulers prove ephemeral, swept away by the awful consequences of a myopia which seems endemic. Yet for all their manifest failings, the Galfridian Britons dominate events. Their persistent folly may have a more enduring impact than their valour, but they shape the course of Insular history just the same. Unlike his predecessors, Geoffrey ascribed a major, hitherto unsuspected, role to the Britons, and by so doing he forced the twelfth century to reappraise a significant portion of Britain's past.

Geoffrey restricts himself to the period during which the conduct of the Britons might be said to determine – for better and for worse – the course of Insular history. The systematic portion of the account extends down to the death of Cadwaladr in 689, a point nearly two and a half centuries after the juncture previously used to mark the effective beginning of Anglo-Saxon rule. Without exception pre-Galfridian writers treat the arrival of Hengist and Horsa, traditionally assigned to the year 449, as the dividing line. More than half the *Historia*, including the Arthurian segment, deals with the period between the famous Saxon landing and Cadwaladr's demise. In other words, much of Geoffrey's reassessment of the Britons' importance takes place at the expense of the Anglo-Saxons. That he was able to propose such a radically different periodization depends both on the character of the Germanic take-over and on the meagre data provided by earlier authorities.

The passage of dominion from the Britons to the Anglo-Saxons cannot be assigned to a specific date. There is no cataclysmic event to provide a sharp demarcation between two eras in the island's history. The developments which culminated in Germanic control of Britain's heartlands span several centuries, and lack the historical definition conducive to precise periodization.[1]

Beginning around the middle of the third century AD, marauding bands of Germanic seafarers exerted mounting pressure on Britain's eastern and southern coasts. The frequency and severity of the raids prompted the Romans to construct an extensive system of defenses along the so-called Saxon Shore.[2] This piratical activity was only one of many internal and external threats to the Empire during the period. It became more and more difficult to administer so remote a province, especially when Continental crises and ambitious commanders gradually pared down the Roman military presence there. The deterioration of local defensive capabilities did not go undetected by probing barbarian peoples who had long harassed lowland Britain. The Pictish incursion of 367 is only one notable example of renewed raiding activity. Sometime before the end of the fourth century, British authority apparently found it necessary to settle groups of Saxon federates in particularly vulnerable or strategically important areas. Such officially sanctioned buffer-colonies had worked well elsewhere in the Empire, and may have given the Britons some initial respite from attack. The benefits of this arrangement, however, proved short-lived, as the Saxon mercenaries turned against their Celtic overlords.

The former federates seem to have been joined by more recent arrivals from the Continent and to have pushed inland in discrete bands which probably comprised only the followers of minor leaders. Although smaller groups undoubtedly tended to merge into more viable military and economic units, the Anglo-Saxon penetration was hesitant. Germanic settlers gained effective control of the rich lowlands only gradually, as domination proceeded outward from small enclaves established over a considerable period of time. This piecemeal conquest is remarkable for its persistence, rather than for its decisiveness. The Anglo-Saxons would continue to expand their domain, but never subjugated the entire island. The Britons were left in control of the remoter hill districts, while the nascent English kingdoms turned their energies against each other in a struggle for supremacy. The borders with the Celts required frequent adjustment and defense, but the fact remains that the initial period of conquest gave way almost imperceptibly to a time of consolidation.

Modern perceptions of the Anglo-Saxon rise to pre-eminence depend heavily upon archaeological evidence, a source of information denied medieval historians. A Gildas or a Bede might note the most obvious vestiges of the Romano-British past, but lacked the basic knowledge for dating and interpreting such physical remnants. Antiquities served to corroborate data found in oral traditions or written accounts, and possessed no independent value for reconstructing the probable course of events. Because the source materials bearing on early Insular history were exceedingly sparse, the necessity of correlating archaeological evidence with historical report inevitably produced and perpetuated erroneous associations. The handling of the Hadrianic Wall offers a notorious example.[3] Gildas and Bede found it possible to interpret cultural remains only within the framework of available narrative sources. When standard authority or venerable tradition contained no mention, then the survivals of an earlier era could not be assigned a specific place in Britain's history. The Roman roads and buildings still visible in Bede's day bore witness to a well-attested occupation (HE, 1.11, p 40), but the importance of such construction for the administration and defense of the island at any given time could not be inferred. Certainly it proved impossible to connect coastal defenses or other fortifications with incursions by Germanic peoples.

Down to Henry of Huntingdon's day, medieval notions regarding the passage of dominion derive almost entirely from meagre data which seldom attest more than later traditions. Neither the Britons nor the Anglo-Saxons left contemporary records of the early Germanic efforts to gain a foothold on the island. Approximately one hundred and fifty years separate the first federate settlements from the composition of the *De excidio et conquestu Britanniae*.[4] Although Gildas does provide contemporary testimony for events of the first half of the sixth century, his didactic concerns severely limit the amount of historical data supplied. Continental sources are more numerous and generally fuller for the period in question, but these texts rarely note Insular occurrences. The Germanic take-over of Britain attracted little contemporary notice on the Continent, and subsequent accounts of the landings and settlements would be drawn perforce from Insular traditions, most of which were transmitted orally for centuries before being recorded. There is a strong presumption that a substantial proportion, perhaps even the majority, of such materials failed to reach later historians, but how extensive this body of traditional lore might once have been remains unclear. Gildas and Bede seem to possess specific information only for Hengist and Horsa, a fact which has very definite consequences for historiographic depictions.

In medieval accounts the Saxons intrude upon Insular affairs with dramatic suddenness. Gildas is the principal written source for the turbulent years which followed the end of the Roman occupation, and his views would pass via Bede into most subsequent depictions. In the *De excidio* there is no mention of the Saxons nor any hint of a threat from the Continent prior to the famous landing by three ships carrying the followers of Hengist and Horsa. Indeed, these warriors reputedly undertook the voyage at the invitation of the Britons (DEB, c 23, pp 38–9). Although Bede adds important details to the story, he does not alter the abruptness with which Germanic involvement in Britain's history begins (HE, 1.14–15, pp 48–50).[5] In retrospect both writers impute ambitious designs to the first Saxon arrivals, but there is no sense that this landing must be seen in the context of earlier raids by marauding bands of Germanic seafarers.

The tale of the fateful British invitation is set against the backdrop of repeated attacks launched by the Irish and the Picts. At the time of the first Saxon landing the Britons are depicted as preoccupied with this long-standing threat. According to Gildas, the incursions from the north began at the close of the fourth century, after Magnus Maximus had stripped Britain of soldiery in pursuit of his Continental ambitions (DEB, c 14, p 33. Cf Bede, HE, 1.12, p 40). On three separate occasions the pressure from the Irish and the Picts became so intense that the Britons turned to Rome for military aid. The first two appeals brought prompt intervention and some respite, but the third proved to be in vain.[6] Denied Roman assistance and faced with renewed attacks from the north, help was sought among the Continent's Germanic tribes. The Saxon mercenaries, who responded to the invitation, are said to have been settled in the east to provide a buffer between the Britons and their northern foes (DEB, c 23, p 38; HE, 1.15, p 50). The depredations of the Irish and the Picts dominate accounts of the half-century preceding the arrival of Hengist and Horsa.

Any awareness of the continuity of Saxon involvement in Britain's history appears to have been lost well before Gildas' day. No Insular writer from the sixth through the twelfth century is cognizant of the fact that Germanic seafarers pillaged towns and disrupted commerce for some two hundred years prior to Vortigern's fateful invitation. Eutropius' *Breviarium*, a work familiar to Bede and many other medieval writers, contains one of the earliest references to Saxon piracy.[7] The passage in question, however, deals principally with the Roman admiral Carausius, who was in command of the English Channel and set himself up as emperor in Britain, only to be murdered in 293. Eutropius does not explicitly associate the Saxons with Britain, and in the absence of any other information it would be well-nigh impossible to connect Carausius' career with Germanic pressure along the Saxon Shore. Bede makes no reference to this section of the *Breviarium*.

Gildas and then Bede report that when the Romans responded to the second British appeal for help, watchtowers were constructed along the south coast in an effort to safeguard the shipping lanes from barbarian attacks (DEB, c 18, p 35; HE, 1.12, p 44). The reference undoubtedly should be connected with the rebuilding of older fortifications along the Saxon Shore,[8] but Gildas and Bede seem to regard the construction as noteworthy, because new. Like the stone wall erected by the Romans at the same time, this defensive measure has become necessary in consequence of the Britons' demonstrated inability to protect their island homeland. The earthen rampart, constructed earlier by the Britons, proved ineffectual, because the Irish and the Picts merely sailed around this fortified line, outflanking the defenders (DEB, c 16, pp 33–4; HE, 1.12, p 42). Not only did the Britons build the wrong type of wall, they failed to take the possibility of so obvious a manoeuvre into account. Now the Romans must rectify both shortcomings, providing a proper system of defenses across the northern border and along the coast. This construction activity remains within the context of the Hiberno-Pictish invasions. Gildas and Bede are totally unaware that the Saxons constituted a major threat at this or any earlier juncture.

The abruptness with which the Germanic threat revealed itself made the arrival of Hengist and Horsa an obvious turning point in Insular history. The three boatloads of mercenaries, however, had not conquered Britain in a single campaign. The actual passage of dominion had to fall at some later point, but the progress of the Anglo-Saxons proved difficult to chart. Neither Gildas nor Bede is able to assign any specific occurrence to the first fifty years of the Germanic presence.

Gildas describes in general terms the savagery of Saxon raids during this period, but the account lacks detail. The British villages and churches sacked by the Germanic invaders are not identified, and he says nothing of the location, size, and history of the eastern enclaves from which the Saxons launched these attacks. After ravaging the Britons' domain, the plunderers would return to their settlements, thereby leaving in doubt the extent of the territory actually seized in such operations (DEB, cc 24–5, pp 39–40).

Bede moves directly from the account of the first landing to his famous comments on the arrivals of the Angles, the Saxons, and the Jutes (HE, 1.15, pp 50–2). The description seems to imply large-scale invasions, but it must be remembered that in the absence of specific details Bede has compressed a half-century of Insular history into a very small space. Events have been telescoped, making this section of the *Historia ecclesiastica* a counterpoise to the *Anglo-Saxon Chronicle*, in which the mechanical arrangement of materials produces artificial protraction.[9] Bede's handling of the *adventus* bespeaks little more than cognizance of an initial period of Anglo-Saxon expansion, one in which actual gains were impossible to assess.

Although the second half of the fifth century was thought to have witnessed significant growth by permanent Germanic settlements, the end of this period did not find the Anglo-Saxons in complete control of the heartlands. Bede had no reason to doubt Gildas' statement that after Ambrosius Aurelianus rallied the Britons from their initial unpreparedness, first one side and then the other emerged victorious (DEB, cc 25–6, p 40; HE, 1.16, p 54). After some fifty years of dimly perceived struggles, the first specific event reported by either man is the Battle of Mount Badon, a stunning British triumph (DEB, c 26, p 40; HE, 1.16, pp 52–4).[10] On Gildas' unimpeachable authority, early Anglo-Saxon expansion had been followed by a lengthy period during which the Britons held the invaders in check. Bede lacked any evidence to the contrary, and indeed the balance of political power was of secondary importance to him. From Bede's point of view the real struggle for the island's future would be waged by representatives of the apostolic faith, beginning with Augustine's arrival in 597.[11]

In marked contrast to the *Historia ecclesiastica*, the *Anglo-Saxon Chronicle* focuses almost exclusively on the political history of the early enclaves. The first fifty years of the Germanic presence are no longer a virtual blank, but rather have been filled out with entries on specific landings and battles. Several encounters between the Britons and the invaders are assigned to the second half of the fifth century, and on each occasion the Anglo-Saxons triumph.[12] The Battle of Mount Badon is suppressed entirely, and the reason can perhaps be inferred with some degree of certainty. The West Saxon bias of the *Chronicle* has long been recognized, and any notice of the British victory at Mount Badon would have to be inserted right around the time of Cerdic's arrival. Such an entry would inevitably detract from the significance of the landing, and raise doubts about the accomplishments of the man credited with founding the kingdom of Wessex. Through the judicious selection and arrangement of materials Anglo-Saxon expansion is made to appear in the *Chronicle* as a steadily rising curve.

Although the English victories convey a sense of military dominance and uninterrupted progress, the *Anglo-Saxon Chronicle* offers no firm foundation for precise periodization. Epochal significance is never attached to any single campaign; indeed the nature of the recorded encounters would seem to preclude such importance. All the early battles pit the Britons not against a unified Germanic host, but against armies put in the field by individual enclaves. The entire question of co-ordinated military operations by the Anglo-Saxons is extremely vexed. Certainly the *Chronicle* provides no indication of a combined effort, from which the advent of English rule might be dated. Centuries separate the actual events from the written records, and presumably only the memory of major battles could have survived the perils of transmission across so great a time-span. Historical importance, however, is a relative judgment, dependent upon the context in which events and personages are placed. In the *Anglo-Saxon Chronicle* the entries for the second half of the fifth century and first half of the sixth tend to define the significance of any given occurrence in relation to the history of a single enclave. This feature of the account should doubtless be attributed to the fact that the compilers incorporated a substantial number of regional traditions.

Nevertheless, the perspective of the *Chronicle* is considerably broader than that which would have marked source materials bearing on a specific district. Such a compilation presupposes that the several regional histories form part of a larger picture, but the annalists could not move beyond their sources to assess the immediate consequences of specific events for the passage of dominion. Nor would any later writer be able to single out a particular campaign as marking a decisive turning point in Insular history. The gathering together of discrete traditions failed to confer historical insight which was in any way commensurate with the scope of the depiction. For this reason the *Anglo-Saxon Chronicle* remains a compilation of narrow viewpoints and does not provide a coherent overview of the Germanic conquest of Britain. West Saxon affairs do, to be sure, loom large in the entries from 495 onwards, but the importance of Wessex is not inferred from the sketchy information contained in these annals.

For events which transpired after the mid-sixth century, the crucial junctures were better defined. The principal sources remained Bede and the *Anglo-Saxon Chronicle*, but the data became more plentiful and the outlines of English history much sharper. Of paramount importance for historiographic depiction was the fact that the material changes touched not only the quantity and coherence of the available information. When the image began to clear, the focus was no longer on the struggle between the Britons and the Anglo-Saxons for control of the island. In Bede's *Historia ecclesiastica* the emphasis fell on Augustine's mission and the progress of the apostolic faith, while the *Anglo-Saxon Chronicle* charted the competition for supremacy among the nascent English kingdoms. Insular history obviously had entered a new phase, but the previous epoch had ended without giving notice of its passing. The century and a half which separated Augustine from Hengist and Horsa was devoid of those historical markers normally used for periodization. The first Saxon landing stood out in sharp relief, but the record of subsequent events failed to yield a sharp division between two eras which were perceived as very distinctive in character.

The inability to fix the passage of dominion did not obscure the fact that Britain had undergone significant change in consequence of the Germanic take-over. The years which followed establishment of the first permanent settlements had witnessed the gradual emergence of Anglo-Saxon England from the Romano-British past. Even in the twelfth century a writer need not look far for evidence of the continuing importance of this transition. Despite the Danish and Norman invasions, the system of geographical divisions in common usage still attested to landings by bands of Germanic warriors. No catalogue of England's identifying features could avoid mention of events in the fifth and sixth centuries.[13] The surviving records might make precise periodization impossible, but the vagaries of the sources could not dim awareness of the profound cultural changes which the landings had produced.

For medieval writers the Anglo-Saxons constituted a cultural entity distinct in language and custom from the Celts. The separation could be read in Britain's toponymy, and was a very real factor in the policy-making of England's rulers. Historiographers imputed a fairly high degree of ethnic homogeneity to the Anglo-Saxons, and superimposed this sense of unity on the political fragmentation of the fifth and sixth centuries. There can be little doubt that in the absence of precise ethnological information, writers projected the circumstances of their own day backward through time. That Britain had been invaded by three Germanic peoples and not by one was familiar from Bede, but the famous description contained nothing on the specific differences between these tribes (HE, 1.15, p 50).[14] The identifying features, which once may have distinguished the Angles, the Saxons, and the Jutes from each other, left no trace in the Middle Ages. Writers could only judge the importance of the tribal groupings on the basis of subsequent events, and the evidence did not indicate a major impact. On the contrary, any survey of English history suggested the long-term significance of those elements which tended to unify the invaders. The Anglo-Saxon domain remained badly fragmented, but these divisions were seen as political, rather than tribal in origin.

Given the nature of the sources, the notion of an underlying cultural unity was of limited practical value for historiographic depiction. Medieval writers lacked sufficient data to structure their accounts around this perception. The conversion of the Anglo-Saxons began with the events of 597, and information on the pagan culture, which had flourished for some hundred and fifty years prior to Augustine's mission, was non-existent. For the fifth and sixth centuries only the histories of the several enclaves could be discerned. Although there can be no doubting the importance of these territorial units, it is well to remember that the vestiges of local traditions are an expression of conscious efforts to achieve and maintain political identity. Whatever the awareness of a common Germanic heritage may have been, the source materials available to Bede and the compilers of the *Chronicle* accentuated existing divisions. The first centuries of Anglo-Saxon rule simply could not be depicted as the evolution of a monolithic cultural entity. The course of events was comprehensible only in terms of discrete lines of history, generated by a group of seemingly autonomous enclaves. In the extant sources individual settlements could be seen to grow through the annexation of surrounding territories, gradually taking on political definition. From the first Germanic enclaves emerged the Anglo-Saxon kingdoms, institutional manifestations of vested interests which in many cases probably stemmed from the character of the invasions. Some settlements never reached this stage, while for others the period of independence would be all too brief. The several lines differed greatly in length, but each contributed data to the overall picture.

The early recorded histories of the enclaves consisted of little more than regnal lists. Neither the age nor the accuracy of these royal genealogies is at issue here, but only their impact on historiographic depictions of fifth- and sixth-century English rule. The earliest such lists invariably trace the line of succession back to Woden.[15] Insular writers exhibit considerable uncertainty as to the identity of this figure and frequently speculate on the reason for Woden's importance to Germanic kingship.[16] Despite the manifest confusion, there can be no doubt that the pedigrees represent a familiar form of dynastic propaganda. The enumeration of a king's illustrious ancestry, especially a line of descent which includes a deity, serves to legitimize the claim to sovereignty.[17] The Anglo-Saxon genealogies bespeak a desire on the part of individual enclaves to establish political identity. Each wished to be regarded as a discrete entity, one which merited consideration in its own right, and the materials passed on to succeeding generations reflected these aspirations. The settlements laid claim to their several histories, and endeavoured to maintain that degree of distinctiveness upon which ultimately political survival depended. The data generated in conjunction with these efforts would long outlive the actual kingdoms, forcing a highly differentiated image on later historians.

For twelfth-century historiographers the beginnings of the Anglo-Saxon period could be perceived only in terms of essentially discrete enclaves. The fragmentation of early English rule may be historically accurate, but the data available tended to heighten the sense of separateness where these nascent kingdoms were concerned. The somewhat exaggerated image resulted not only from the nature of the material on the Germanic settlements themselves. The histories of the several enclaves so dominated events of the fifth and sixth centuries, because the indigenous Celts were barely discernible in the accounts of standard authorities.

Prior to the appearance of Geoffrey of Monmouth's *Historia regum Britanniae*, the Anglo-Saxon kingdoms existed in a vacuum created by the almost complete absence of information bearing on the Britons. The Celtic response to gradual Germanic expansion simply could not be charted in any detail. Except for the victory at Mount Badon, there was little of a specific nature to suggest the effectiveness of presumed British countermeasures. Gildas did, to be sure, describe a rather considerable period during which the Anglo-Saxons were held in check, but his testimony produced no balanced assessments of the relative strengths of the contending peoples.

Unlike later writers, Gildas did not regard Anglo-Saxon ascendancy as the inevitable outcome of the struggle for control of the island. He was acutely aware of the threat posed by the Germanic presence, a danger which his fellow Britons persistently compounded by their own folly. The British resurgence had brought comparative peace to the land, but, instead of seizing the moment, the Britons had lapsed into indolence and even depravity. Nevertheless, the calm gave cause for hope. It was not too late. A chance for significant advance lay at hand, if the Britons would only abandon their profligate ways. Despite the harshness of the characterization, Gildas' didacticism rests on a fundamentally optimistic belief in the educability of his countrymen.

In order to achieve the desired result, Gildas' contemporaries must be made to see both the nature of their folly and the historical ramifications of persistent myopia. Toward this end he reviews past and present failings, largely ignoring the deeds of the valiant or the virtuous. The technique is a familiar one, but the historical data selected for inclusion serve only the didactic purpose.[18] Gildas is not a systematic historian and a very small portion of the *De excidio* can be termed 'historical,' even in a limited sense. The vast preponderance of the text is homiletic, and this is especially true of the sections which deal with conditions in his own day. He has no intention of providing a comprehensive record of contemporary events. The victory at Mount Badon, which coincided with the year of his birth (DEB, c 26, p 40), is the last event treated in the *De excidio*.[19] Gildas' preoccupations are understandable, but the loss of what he might have reported would prove irretrievable. Neither the *Historia Brittonum* nor the sparse entries of British annalists adequately cover the time-span in question.[20] Even taken together, these sources do not yield a coherent outline and chronological framework comparable to what is available in the *Anglo-Saxon Chronicle*. During the period which witnessed the passage of dominion, the activities of the Britons remain obscure.

For succeeding generations of pre-Galfridian writers the prevailing view of the fifth and sixth centuries was a composite drawn almost exclusively from Bede and the *Anglo-Saxon Chronicle*. Nevertheless, the contours of the *De excidio* constitute an important feature of these historiographic depictions, owing to the fact that Bede relied heavily on the Gildasian survey of Insular history. Bede first incorporated the *De excidio* into the *Chronica majora* (to 725), and some appreciation of his debt to Gildas can be gained from a comparison with the earlier *Chronica minora* (to 703). It was the *Historia ecclesiastica* (completed in 731), however, which later proved a useful complement to the political history fashioned by English annalists in the *Anglo-Saxon Chronicle*.

Bede's handling of the peace following Mount Badon offers an instructive example of how writers came to discount the Britons as a significant factor in the struggle for control of the island.

The *De excidio* is Bede's principal source of information on Insular affairs down through the victory at Mount Badon (HE, 1.16, pp 52–4; DEB, cc 25–6, p 40). After reporting the triumph, Bede does not continue with temporal developments, but rather inserts a lengthy account of Germanus' successful efforts to check the spread of Pelagianism (HE, 1.17–21, pp 54–66). According to Prosper of Aquitaine, the bishop of Auxerre first visited Britain in 429,[21] and Bede acknowledges that it will be necessary to go back in time to a point a few years before the arrival of Hengist and Horsa. The famous landing has already been assigned to the approximate midpoint of the fifth century (HE, 1.15, p 48), and Bede takes Gildas' comment on the relative chronology to mean that the Battle of Mount Badon was fought some forty-four years after the first band of Saxons set foot on the island (HE, 1.16, p 54; DEB, c 26, p 40). This would seem to place the British victory in the last decade of the fifth century. To return to the time of Germanus' initial visit requires a rather considerable jump backwards. The events in question may be only two decades earlier than the arrival of Hengist and Horsa, but this Saxon landing is not the last occurrence depicted prior to insertion of the material on Germanus. Bede interrupts the chronological sequence after recounting the British triumph at Mount Badon. A chronological leap of sixty or seventy years is at issue. Bede seems conscious of the fact that after such a major victory some discussion of the aftermath is in order, and he breaks with the promise to report more on the subject later: 'Sed haec postmodum' (HE, 1.16, p 54).

Following the depiction of Germanus' career, Bede does in fact return to the period after Mount Badon. He picks up the chronological thread with a close paraphrase of Gildas' remarks on the peace which resulted from the British triumph (HE, 1.22, pp 66–8; DEB, c 26, pp 40–1). The account resumes right where Bede abandoned the *De excidio* to insert the material on Germanus. Indeed, despite the length of the intervening section, the paraphrase begins with Gildas' very next sentence. A simple *interea* is added to mask the actual chronology; then Bede rehearses Gildas' general comments on the aftermath. So long as the memory of the trials which preceded Mount Badon remained fresh, the effects of peace were salutary. However, sin and corruption became rife, when a generation grew up knowing only comparative tranquillity. At this juncture Gildas turns to the character of British rule (DEB, c 27, p 41), but Bede does not follow. The focus shifts instead to the history of Insular Christianity. Bede states that among the Britons' sins, 'quae historicus eorum Gildas flebili sermone describit' (HE, 1.22, p 68), must be numbered the failure of the British

Church to undertake the conversion of the Anglo-Saxons. Mention of this subject serves as a transition to the background of Augustine's mission (HE, 1.23, p 68).

What underlies Bede's selectivity in the use of data from the *De excidio* is a fundamentally different view of developments in the fifth and sixth centuries. For Gildas the British resurgence marked an epoch in Insular history. The peace which followed had endured and had had an insidiously corrupting effect on an entire generation. The conduct of these same Britons would shape the future course of events, and Gildas could only warn of the danger inherent in persistent folly. He had to rely upon the combined force of Insular precedent and biblical parallel, because the ramifications of observable failings extended beyond the range of his apprehension. Gildas hoped for a timely reversal of contemporary trends, but Bede could see the ultimate outcome. The military equilibrium enjoyed by the Britons had proved to be only temporary. Once the struggle for control of the heartlands had been decided, there was little to be gained by rehearsing Gildas' catalogue of the symptoms of a British decline.[22] The accomplished fact would be expected to take precedence, and did. Bede had no Anglo-Saxon victory which might serve to counterbalance Mount Badon and to mark a turning point in the second half of the sixth century. On the other hand, he did not see alternations in the fortunes of war as crucial to the island's future. From Bede's point of view only Augustine's mission possessed truly epoch-making significance. He looked past the aftermath of a notable British triumph to events nearly a century later.

Bede selected his data with full benefit of historical hindsight. What he took to be the long-term consequences of Augustine's arrival made this event of greater relative importance than the comparatively brief British resurgence. Bede's personal bias should not be allowed to obscure the underlying process at work. Where the distant past is concerned, decisions regarding the inclusion of specific items depend upon an assessment of the ramifications. Because the historical impact of a given event or personage becomes increasingly clear with the passage of time, it follows that fewer and fewer specifics will be adjudged important for an understanding of what follows. Details which are non-essential to the perceived significance tend to fall away in subsequent historiographic depictions. Bede's own account of Augustine's mission would suffer the same fate. Succeeding generations of historians eliminated much of the material on the Easter controversy as irrelevant to an understanding of the course of events.

The treatment accorded the first Saxon landing offers an instructive comparison with the handling of Mount Badon. It can perhaps be assumed that the news of a major battle attracted more immediate notice than the arrival of a band of

Saxon mercenaries. Yet the consequences of a seemingly minor incident proved to be of far greater significance than those of a stunning victory.[23] This fact is clearly reflected in the transmission of data bearing on the two events. Traditions regarding Hengist and Horsa were repeated and elaborated throughout the Middle Ages. No account of early Insular history was complete without consideration of the landing and what followed. The British victory at Mount Badon did, to be sure, receive historiographic notice, but to the eyes of later historians the battle seemed only a momentary reprieve. Gildas supplied significant details both on the duration of the peace following Mount Badon and on the failings of the Britons during this same period. The information in the *De excidio* might have provided an important corrective to the English viewpoint, but it quickly disappeared, owing largely to Bede's selectivity. The difference between the historiographic fates of Mount Badon and the first Saxon landing depended ultimately upon a judgment passed on the ramifications of the two events in question.

What happened in the case of the *De excidio* points up an important fact. The surviving data from remote eras do not necessarily mirror the balance of power at any given moment. English chroniclers, writing well after the events in question, give little indication that the victory at Mount Badon was more than an isolated military reversal; but according to Gildas, the battle formed part of a general resurgence which freed the Britons from Saxon pressure for half a century, perhaps even longer. What appeared as a temporary shift to later historians actually dominated Gildas' entire lifetime. Similar realignments may have disappeared without a trace, but writers can perhaps be forgiven for drawing a different conclusion.

The availability of data on the early history of a people depends upon countless factors, any and all of which may distort prevailing views. Although not averse to correcting misconceptions, medieval historians seldom found themselves in a position to divine what lay behind patterns of transmission. In the case of the Britons both the quantity and the character of surviving data seemed to deny this Celtic people a positive role in determining the shape of Insular history. The information was, to be sure, not evenly distributed. The first millennium of the British presence remained an intriguing blank, one which defied the efforts of pre-Galfridian writers. So far as anyone knew, the kings of the Britons from Brutus to Cassibellaunus had ruled over an independent land, but the subsequent course of events must have raised doubts as to the level of attainment reached during this period. Whatever accomplishments there may have been had had no lasting effect, an inference seemingly corroborated by the silence of Continental authorities. When the activities of the Britons did become discernible in available sources, nothing was so apparent as their feebleness and folly. At three crucial junctures these Celts had been unable to defend their homeland against foreign incursion, thereby forfeiting any claim to pre-eminence in Insular affairs. First the Romans, then the Irish and the Picts, and finally Continental Germanic tribes had given direction to Britain's history.

Taken by itself, the fact that the island fell under Roman domination said little about the indigenous Britons. Much of the civilized world had at some point suffered the same fate. Moreover, the Empire was seen in a generally favourable light, through the eyes of men like Orosius and Eutropius. With the end of Roman administration, however, the Britons displayed a shocking degree of military ineptitude, and seemed in every regard an enfeebled people. This view derived ultimately from Gildas, who was the only source of information on the British response to the Hiberno-Pictish and Anglo-Saxon threats.[24] Throughout the period of recorded Insular history the pattern seemed clear. It was the invaders who had shaped the future, while the Britons merely reacted, apparently unaware of the long-term consequences of their deeds. Gildas' most important legacy to later historians was a uniformly negative interpretation of the scant materials available.

During the Middle Ages Gildas was more revered than read. The *De excidio* does not seem to have enjoyed wide circulation, and the mistaken attribution of the *Historia Brittonum* to Gildas bespeaks considerable uncertainty regarding the work upon which his reputation as a historian rested.[25] Bede drew heavily on the *De excidio*, thereby ensuring that selected items would become canonical. The specific borrowings, however, did not appear under Gildas' name. Bede felt under no obligation to acknowledge his indebtedness to standard authorities with any regularity. In the eighth century frequent source references simply were not a feature of the two historiographic traditions represented by the *Chronica majora* and the *Historia ecclesiastica*. Bede mentioned Gildas only once, characterizing him in the *Historia ecclesiastica* as a British *historicus* who had enumerated the sins of his own countrymen (HE, 1.22, p 68). The reference occurs at the end of brief comments on the aftermath of Mount Badon and serves as a transition to the background for Augustine's mission.

Generally speaking, later writers connect the name of Gildas with the decline of the Britons in the period following the Saxon landings. This association accurately reflects the didactic concern of the *De excidio*, but bears no relationship to the historical data actually borrowed. The materials derived from Gildas deal predominantly with events down through the arrival of Hengist and Horsa, a fact which could not be inferred from Bede. Except for the Battle of Mount Badon, virtually nothing on the post-invasion era was taken from Gildas, and even his account of this British triumph would be supplanted by the

Arthurian version found in the *Historia Brittonum* (HB, c 56, p 200). Thanks both to Bede and to the apparent scarcity of the *De excidio*, Gildas enjoyed a reputation which was largely independent of specific data.

Despite unavoidable misconceptions regarding the contents of the *De excidio*, medieval assessments of the Britons' position in the sixth century depend ultimately on Gildas. He exercised a considerable influence, even though his testimony pertaining to this period failed to find inclusion in standard sources. Prevailing notions rested not on specific data contained in the *De excidio*, but rather on inferences drawn from Gildas' overall view of British history. The hope which he had held out for the aftermath of Mount Badon disappeared with Bede's selection of materials, leaving only the litany of earlier British follies. Nevertheless, the interpretation which later writers placed on the outlines of Insular history was entirely consistent with the *De excidio*, and in fact represented an extension of the viewpoint enunciated therein. Gildas had passed over the deeds of valorous Britons, because their exploits had not determined the shape of events. British folly had proved a far more potent force in shaping the island's past, and Gildas feared that the opportunity presented by the Britons' latest resurgence would go the way of earlier achievements. To Bede the Anglo-Saxon ascendancy seemed proof that this had taken place. For the most part unwittingly, subsequent generations adopted a view which was in essence an extrapolation from Gildas' didactic framework.

Twelfth-century writers inserted the British triumph at Mount Badon into the list of Anglo-Saxon victories reported in the *Chronicle*. Although completely isolated in this context, the battle possessed a special fascination, one which belied its apparent lack of long-term historical significance. Interest in the battle, however, stemmed not from a general reassessment of the relative strengths of the contending peoples, but rather from an important change in personalia. Between Bede's day and the ninth century, when the *Historia Brittonum* was compiled, a reason had been found for the dramatic, albeit short-lived upturn in British fortunes. Arthur's name had become associated with Mount Badon, and his leadership was seen as crucial to the triumph. Though distrustful of Arthur's popular reputation, William of Malmesbury suspected that the career of this British commander might have been marked by greater distinction than was evident from the entries of chroniclers (GRA, 1.8, 1:11–12). William was drawn to the well-attested resurgence by Arthur's obvious appeal and not by scepticism regarding the conventional view of sixth-century Insular history. Even if, as the *Historia Brittonum* would have it, the Britons under Arthur's command never suffered a defeat (HB, c 56, p 200), the outcome of the struggle for control of the island remained unchanged. The military accomplishments of the fabled Arthur had provided only a brief respite, and raised no fundamental doubts as to the validity of traditional interpretations.

Where fifth- and sixth-century Insular history was concerned, the distribution and general character of the data seemed to admit of only one interpretation. The Britons had continued to dwell on the island after the Germanic invasions, but were a negligible force in determining the future course of events. Given the fact that the *De excidio* had provided the underlying framework for the prevailing view of British potential, the inference was logical, indeed almost inevitable. Since the time of the Roman occupation invading peoples had shaped Insular history, irrespective of whether they had settled permanently in the heartlands. For all practical purposes the first intrusion of a foreign power could be taken as marking the beginning of a new era.[26] Hengist and Horsa may have brought only a small band of warriors, but there was absolutely no indication that the Britons need be taken into serious account when considering the passage of dominion.

With the exception of Æthelweard's truncated chronicle, the years which separate Bede from the Norman Conquest are dominated by annalistic writings.[27] The periodization of early Insular history remained unproblematic for two principal reasons: 1/ no new information came to light on the Britons, and 2/ the dominant mode of historiographic depiction did not entail the schematization of data. The situation was static, and writers paid little attention to the transition from British to Anglo-Saxon rule. Geoffrey of Monmouth would eventually alter the Britons' image, but historiographic preferences changed first.

The first half of the twelfth century witnessed a revival of interest in large-scale surveys of Insular history. The activity is a tacit acknowledgment of how much remained to be done in systematizing the data and depicting the course of events. This concern for the overall shape of developments might be expected to draw attention to the Britons and to problems of periodization. Initially, however, writers exhibit little inclination even to marshal the available pre-Saxon materials. Some background on Vortigern's invitation was deemed necessary, but only because the Britons' feebleness had cleared the way for the Germanic conquest. William of Malmesbury's opening sentence deals with Hengist and Horsa. A brief survey of the Roman and sub-Roman periods does follow, but William clearly regards English history as comprehensible without a detailed discussion of the Britons (GRA, 1.1–4, 1:5–8). The *Worcester Chronicle* sketches the outlines of universal history, but devotes no space to Celtic rule. For the pre-Saxon era this work rehearses only the entries of its source, the universal chronicle of Marianus Scotus.[28] Practically speaking, the interpolation of data into Marianus' framework starts with the landing of Hengist and Horsa.[29] At about the same time the F-text of the *Anglo-Saxon*

Chronicle does make some use of the *Historia Brittonum*. The Brutus story is included, but very little else.[30] The borrowings remain highly selective and do not bear on events of the fifth and sixth centuries.[31] As in other manuscripts of the *Anglo-Saxon Chronicle*, no mention is made either of Mount Badon or of Arthur.

Henry of Huntingdon is the first writer to assemble the available data on the Britons.[32] His efforts bespeak the conviction that Insular history must be regarded as a whole, even if the emphasis would eventually fall on the English and Anglo-Norman periods. Relevant materials were gleaned from Bede, the *Historia Brittonum*, and various Continental historians. The amount of information, however, was not sufficient to force reconsideration of the conventional periodization. The entire question of when the passage of dominion took place remained unaffected by the infusion of data. In the *Historia Anglorum* the arrival of Hengist and Horsa marks the advent of a new era (HA, 2.1, pp 37–8). Although the physical presence of a band of Saxon warriors would hardly seem to constitute a military take-over, the Britons all but disappear from Henry's account following the first landing. The available pre-Saxon materials were not enough to offset Anglo-Saxon traditions.

Geoffrey of Monmouth's *Historia regum Britanniae* altered the situation dramatically and created a problem in periodization peculiar to the twelfth century. Writers were suddenly faced not only with a wealth of detailed information on the Britons, but also with an overt challenge to prevailing notions regarding the passage of dominion. Geoffrey extended the period during which the Britons constituted the dominant force in Insular affairs well into what was normally reckoned as belonging to Anglo-Saxon history. His account offered an alternative and decidedly British view of events in the fifth, sixth, and even seventh centuries.

With the appearance of the *Historia*, writers in the twelfth century were brought face to face with a startling and very disquieting reality. The conventional periodization did not rest on a secure foundation. So long as only the pre-Galfridian data on the Britons were available, Anglo-Saxon tradition seemed unshakeable. Geoffrey's challenge, however, revealed hitherto unsuspected gaps and weaknesses. For the first time historiographers were forced to justify conventional thinking on the passage of dominion, and found that they could not do so. Some chose to ignore Geoffrey, but those who did draw on the *Historia* had to retreat from the traditional position. The presence of small bands of Saxons no longer sufficed as a marker, and the gradual nature of the take-over left considerable room for uncertainty. The precise location of the dividing line between British and Anglo-Saxon rule became a matter of paramount concern.

The reception accorded Geoffrey's pseudo-history has become a familiar feature of the twelfth century. For a work which purported to be orthodox historiography, the *Historia regum Britanniae* enjoyed unprecedented success. Geoffrey could not have anticipated the popular appeal of his history, but the account obviously struck a very responsive note. In place of the meagre and often unflattering material on the Britons found in other sources, the *Historia* offered a stunning depiction, one which was eagerly received by an age grown conscious of the past.

Geoffrey's achievement cannot be separated from contemporary concern with the shape of Insular history. The entire undertaking presupposed the historiographic activity which had preceded it, and depended upon the limitations of historical methods then in use. Geoffrey of Monmouth knew only too well what progress historians had and had not made, and why. Although the *Historia* challenged many preconceptions, he carefully structured the account to complement the efforts of earlier, as well as contemporary writers. Geoffrey filled the numerous, very sizeable gaps in the record of events for the earliest periods, effectively creating the history of the Britons. Quite obviously any historian who subsequently sought to treat the pre-Saxon era stood to benefit enormously from Geoffrey's supposed recovery of data. Some ambivalence toward the *Historia* would be a recurring feature of the work's reception, but from the thirteenth century onwards Geoffrey's construct provided the standard framework for historiographic depictions of early British history. Such blanket acceptance, however, did not mark the first fifty or sixty years following the appearance of the *Historia*. Geoffrey's account became widely known in a short period of time, but the patterns of historiographic usage are not consistent with the work's popular appeal. Historians of the twelfth century moved very cautiously, and conferred upon Geoffrey only grudgingly the status of acknowledged authority.

Although systematizing the materials of early Insular history was a major preoccupation of writers in England and Normandy, the twelfth century produced very few efforts to incorporate substantial portions of Geoffrey's account into historical surveys. This statistic is revealing but must be interpreted with considerable care. The majority of the works in question are clustered tightly around two points: 1/ mid-century and 2/ the year 1200. Attempts to use the *Historia* as the basis for historiographic depiction of the pre-Saxon era do not disappear in the interim, but the number falls off sharply. The distribution pattern is highly paradoxical and has not received the attention it deserves.

In all likelihood the *Historia regum Britanniae* was completed a year or two before 1139.[33] The first decade after the work's appearance witnessed a spate of activity aimed at integrating Geoffrey's account with more venerable sources, thereby producing a comprehensive overview of the island's past. What William of Malmesbury, the Worcester chronicler, the F-redactor of the *Anglo-Saxon Chronicle*, and Henry of Huntingdon had begun was continued by writers who now could fill the gaps in the pre-Saxon era. The *Historia* generated a great deal of interest among compilers of histories, but usage was by no means universal. Both the enthusiasm and the scepticism would seem natural responses to so new and so startling a depiction. In the second half of the twelfth century the *Historia* was more popular and more readily accessible than it had been prior to 1150. Geoffrey's critics did become vocal, but their number was small, when compared with those who accepted the account as orthodox historiography. The rising curve of public interest, however, did not manifest itself in large-scale historical surveys until the very end of the century. Materials from the *Historia* found many applications, historiographic and otherwise, but efforts to incorporate Geoffrey's depiction into a larger historical context decreased for a time.

Underlying this distribution pattern are historiographic developments which bear directly on how the *Historia* was used. Throughout the twelfth century concern with the relationship of Geoffrey's account to the larger structures of history remained centred in England and Normandy. The text was widely known elsewhere on the Continent, but its popularity stemmed from the material's intrinsic appeal. The matters reported by Geoffrey did not form an integral part of regional history outside the conjoint Anglo-Norman realm, and consequently there was no particular reason to ponder the broader implications of the account. Men like Otto of Freising and the chroniclers of St Denis simply perceived the relevant historical context differently.[34] Historians in England and Normandy, however, began to reorient their own concerns rather soon after 1150. The emphasis shifted away from the large-scale compilations which so dominated the first half of the century. Comprehensive overviews continued to be written, but this type of historical writing ceased to attract the major talents. The leading historians of the day moved increasingly to the depiction of contemporary or near-contemporary events.

The small number of twelfth-century historians to use the framework of the *Historia* depends in large measure on the timing of Geoffrey's composition relative to more general historiographic developments in the Anglo-Norman domain. Only about a decade separates the appearance of the *Historia regum Britanniae* from what has long been seen as an important shift in historical writing.[35] The initial efforts to incorporate the Galfridian construct into a comprehensive survey are heavily concentrated in the ten-year period in question. Prior to about 1150 heavy reliance can be placed on ambitious compilations when assessing the response to Geoffrey's account. In rapid succession several writers take up the problems posed by the *Historia*. Their differing reactions afford considerable insight into the factors tending to limit Geoffrey's reception. During the second half of the century, however, such works no longer constitute a statistically significant part of the contemporary response to the *Historia*. Although the form is hardly moribund, comprehensive overviews cease to reflect either the popularity of Geoffrey's account or the extent of continuing concern with its historical implications.

The leading historians in the third and fourth quarters of the century begin their depictions with events which belong to the Anglo-Norman era. The prevalence of such starting points has an enormous impact on how Geoffrey is used in historiographic contexts. Underlying these choices would appear to be two considerations, probably interrelated. First, the writer's apperception of historical causality seems to be the prime determinant in many cases. He selects a juncture crucial to an understanding of those developments which have shaped the events of his own day.[36] Secondly, the period produced a fairly large number of continuations. This approach to historical writing bespeaks both a willingness to accept the account of a predecessor as authoritative and the belief that the previous generation of systematizers had obviated the need to depict the distant past.[37]

The first half of the twelfth century had in fact produced general agreement on a great many matters, but where Geoffrey of Monmouth was concerned, consensus had been reached only on the problems, not on the solutions. Systematic historians had quickly come to grips with the *Historia*, resolving the manifold difficulties posed by the account in individual and sometimes novel ways. The first decade of the work's reception brought tentative solutions and simple expedients. By mid-century sufficient time had not elapsed for precedents to be established on the handling of certain contentious issues. Trends are identifiable, some of which would form the basis for later conventions, but in the third and fourth quarters of the twelfth century it is much too early to speak of general agreement on the Britons' role in Insular history. The choice of a starting point might eliminate the necessity of dealing with specific problems raised by the *Historia*, but the contemporary focus of historiographic activity in the second half of the twelfth century does not betoken broad-based acceptance of what the preceding generation set in motion. Fundamental issues, all bearing in some way on Geoffrey's veracity, were simply left lying by the major talents of the day. Their accounts dealt with matters far-removed from British and early English history; indeed William of Newburgh was alone in addressing himself to problems which did not bear directly on his depiction.[38] The period witnessed the rise of romance, a development which made itself felt both in the conduct of rulers and in the style used to recount their deeds.[39] Pre-Saxon history and particularly King Arthur fascinated the age, but the continuing response to the challenge represented by the *Historia* cannot be traced through the chronicles of contemporary events.

Geoffrey's depiction, however, did not become history by virtue of its incorporation into chronicles. The *Historia* purported to be conventional historiography and remained the single most important historical document in the spread of the Galfridian construct. The second half of the twelfth century produced enormous interest in the transmission of the text. The *Historia* was copied, edited, and paraphrased with great frequency during this period. Medieval redactors and translators exhibit a notorious penchant for correcting the work at hand. The writers engaged in such activity were acutely aware of the important position which their renderings of a given text occupied in the chain of transmission. Wherever possible, it was encumbent upon them not merely to purvey materials, but to ensure the accuracy of the information. By so doing their endeavour might result in a version which surpassed the original in at least certain regards.

Translators and redactors shared with the systematizers of history an abiding interest in the contours of Geoffrey's depiction. This feature of their work sets them apart from countless others who mined the *Historia* for bits of specific information. But despite the area of common concern, there are substantial methodological differences, the importance of which should not be underestimated. A problem crucial to the compilation of available data can sometimes be ignored with impunity in a vernacular paraphrase or a Latin recension. Translators and redactors, for example, never remark on the absence of corroborating testimony for key sections of the *Historia*, presumably because they were not using standard authorities as a check on Geoffrey's account. Copying, editing, and paraphrasing may alter a text in many ways, but the changes need not result from the weighing of sources and traditions.

Compilers of historical surveys are obliged by the nature of their undertakings to assemble and evaluate available testimony before arriving at a final version of events. Writers engaged in the transmission of a work, especially a history, may also make changes based on a culling of sources. Indeed, Wace serves as a reminder that a twelfth-century translator could be a historian in his own right, one whose familiarity with conventions and standard authorities rivalled that of many of his contemporaries. The *Roman de Brut* and the *Roman de Rou* share numerous features, including a strong romanticizing tendency, but the latter is more obviously a piece of systematic historiography and consciously so.[40] What applies in the case of Wace's two works holds true generally. Irrespective of the accuracy of an account, the underlying methodology possesses much greater visibility in historical compilations than in variant redactions or vernacular paraphrases.

Individual stylistic differences notwithstanding, medieval writers who fashioned overviews of the past are seldom at pains to conceal the methodological underpinnings of their accounts. On the contrary, openness regarding the selection process implies a high order of scrupulousness, which may or may not be justified. Historians who drew heavily on Geoffrey of Monmouth for their depictions of the pre-Saxon era supply impressive lists of the sources consulted, and periodically invoke the names of venerable authorities to warrant the historicity of well-attested events. What goes unsaid is that these standard histories rarely touch the substance of Geoffrey's account. The degree of control possible using earlier writers was more apparent than real. Sufficient data were not available in these sources to provide an effective check on the vast preponderance of material in the *Historia regum Britanniae*. The twelfth century lacked the ability to employ contemporary methods for a searching evaluation of Geoffrey's veracity. At scattered points in the text the absence of supporting evidence raised nagging doubts, but such problems did not admit of ready solution with the means at hand. In most instances acceptance or rejection of Geoffrey's *Historia* was equally subjective, ambivalence merely a sign of ill-defined uneasiness. Even if systematic overviews of Insular history were evenly distributed across the twelfth century, much of the advantage which normally accrues to such writings by virtue of the visibility of the underlying methodology would be lost. In this regard there is little to choose between compilers of compendious surveys on the one hand and redactors and translators on the other.

Investigations tracing the response to Geoffrey's challenge have concentrated on the period after 1300.[41] The fourteenth, fifteenth, and sixteenth centuries produced a large number of efforts to come to grips with the *Historia* in a historiographic context. Against the backdrop of this continuum of usage the great debate over Geoffrey's reliability gradually took shape. This phase of the reception offers a fascinating study in the vicissitudes and ultimate triumph of factual history over Geoffrey's imaginative construct. What differentiates the later centuries from the twelfth is the visibility of the methodological struggle. In the intervening years the *Historia* won acceptance as the standard framework for depictions of the pre-Saxon era. Geoffrey was an acknowledged authority, and anyone wishing to challenge him had to adduce contrary evidence. Not every detail could be refuted, but seventeenth-century critics developed a strong prima facie case which undermined and then toppled the Galfridian construct. At the end of the struggle – some five hundred years after the appearance of the *Historia regum Britanniae* – lies the emergence of something identifiable as the precursor of modern historical methods for treating the pre-Saxon era.

Geoffrey's fall from the ranks of standard authorities is extremely important to the history of historical writing in the early modern period. No one would deny that the initial stages of his reception were just as fateful for medieval historiography, but by and large twelfth-century writers established far-reaching precedents without verifying the accuracy of the *Historia* first. They were unable to do so because of the paucity of controlling data, a fact which precluded the application of contemporary historical methods. For most of the depiction, Geoffrey challenged preconceptions and revised the image of the Britons without contradicting more than the silence of older sources. Late in the account, however, the situation changed dramatically, as may be seen from William of Newburgh's famous denunciation of Geoffrey (HRA, 1: 11–18). William's accusations remain unsubstantiated, until he takes up Geoffrey's assertions regarding the balance of power in seventh-century Britain (HRA, 1: 13–14). Here William of Newburgh finds a significant area of disagreement with Bede's *Historia ecclesiastica* and uses the specifics to justify a general indictment of Geoffrey's veracity.

William was more concerned with a wilful violation of historical ethics than with a potential problem in the periodization of Insular history. To William's way of thinking, the mendacious Geoffrey did not deserve serious consideration, but other twelfth-century writers were reluctant to dismiss the entire account. William of Newburgh was absolutely right about the contradictions and pointed to a section of the *Historia* where the standard methodology might be applied to resolve difficulties. The Galfridian depiction of the sixth and seventh centuries could be checked in part against Bede and the *Anglo-Saxon Chronicle*, thereby making the periodization problem an important test case for medieval historical method. Although earlier writers did not discourse on the significant overlap with other sources, William can hardly lay claim to having discovered its existence. From the outset the post-Arthurian sections of the *Historia* were regarded as highly problematic.

By its very nature the periodization problem might be expected to figure prominently only in the works of historians, whose systematic approach entailed the establishment of chronological divisions. That this is not the case bespeaks both the radical character of Geoffrey's depiction and the strength of prevailing notions. Albeit in different ways, the question of periodization has a palpable impact on historical surveys, vernacular paraphrases, and even on the transmission of the *Historia* itself.

Geoffrey's imaginative account of early British history gained currency soon after its appearance. The Latin text survives in some two hundred manuscripts, and approximately one-quarter of these date from the twelfth century. A Vulgate or Standard Version and two Variant Versions have been identified. Each of the recensions is well attested in the twelfth century; indeed, all three may have circulated during Geoffrey's lifetime.[42] The work's rapid spread has hampered efforts to unravel the complex textual filiations and to establish a relative chronology for the extant versions. The designations First Variant and Second Variant indicate only the order of discovery by modern scholars and not necessarily the order of appearance in the twelfth century.

The priority of the Standard Version has generally been assumed, but in 1957 Robert A. Caldwell expressed the belief that the First Variant represented a pre-Vulgate recension of the *Historia*.[43] He advanced this view in a brief note and provided neither the detailed argumentation nor the supporting evidence required for a hypothesis with such far-reaching implications. Furthermore, although the post-Arthurian segment of the First Variant contains some of the most substantial divergences from the other two recensions, Caldwell's discussion focuses on earlier sections. Certain of the identifying features found in the concluding books involve the periodization problem. Whereas the Vulgate and the Second Variant treat the passage of dominion from the Britons to the Anglo-Saxons in similar fashion,[44] the First Variant does not. Caldwell's thesis bears directly on the selection of a base text for the present study and must be dealt with before proceeding.

The First Variant survives in seven known copies, and these manuscript witnesses may be divided into two categories: 1/ manuscripts which contain a 'pure' variant text, and 2/ manuscripts which conflate the First Variant with the Vulgate.[45] Only the first group is of immediate concern, because the mixed texts share one important feature. Although the method of conflation differs in the various manuscripts, each adopts the Vulgate periodization. Where the passage of dominion is concerned, the 'pure' variant stands completely isolated in the transmission of the *Historia*. Henceforth I will use the designation First Variant only for this text.

In its surviving form the First Variant cannot represent the earliest version of the passage of dominion. What differentiates the periodization in this recension is an attempt to reconcile Anglo-Saxon tradition with a decidedly pro-British view of events.[46] It must be remembered that prior to the appearance of the *Historia regum Britanniae* there was no coherent account of fifth- and sixth-century British rule. When considering the passage of dominion, pre-Galfridian historians ignored the Britons because the available data did not indicate that this people had been a significant factor at so late a date. Before Geoffrey's *Historia* forced the twelfth century to reassess the entire matter, writers had little reason to take the Britons seriously into account, and they certainly had no cause to modify English traditions regarding the importance attached to Hengist and Horsa. The efforts at accommodation found in the First Variant presuppose an earlier version of the *Historia*, one which created a challenge to conventional thinking.

Caldwell's thesis rests on observable differences in the handling of certain sources. The First Variant places greater reliance on authorities such as Bede and Landolfus Sagax, creating the impression of a more conventional compilation process than does the Standard Version. According to Caldwell, the Vulgate redactor introduced the old-book topos, and eliminated selected materials, manipulating the sources in a manner 'consistent with the fiction of the *librum uetustissimum*, of which there is no mention in the Variant' (Caldwell, 'The Use of Sources,' p 124). How this conclusion is to be reconciled with the statement in the preceding paragraph that the Vulgate 'makes greater use of Gildas and Nennius, perhaps at one point even Ordericus Vitalis' eludes me. Caldwell's basic premise, that fundamental differences in the handling of standard authorities hold the key to the relative chronology of the Vulgate and the First Variant, is perfectly valid. Nor can there be any doubt as to the facts, but I do not believe that the patterns indicate the priority of the First Variant.

All assurances to the contrary, the *Historia regum Britanniae* is not orthodox historiography but a carefully wrought piece of pseudo-history. This may be said of all three recensions, and there is every reason to believe that Geoffrey intended his account as a counterbalance to the meagre, often unflattering data available on the Britons in earlier sources. His handling of the Roman period is a case in point. The *Historia* offers a British perspective on events which Bede and Continental authorities recount from the conquerors' point of view. Geoffrey can be seen working against prevailing notions throughout much of the account, and I do not think it reasonable to suppose that he abandoned his infamous methods at scattered junctures to give precedence to those same perspectives which he actively counters elsewhere, especially when key events are involved. Almost certainly the pro-British bias which marks so much of the depiction in the surviving redactions ran throughout the earliest version, as is the case in the Vulgate. All the evidence from the mid-twelfth century points to the prevalence of efforts aimed at reconciling the *Historia* with prior authorities. The First Variant seems to be a product of this general trend and not, as Caldwell would have it, a slightly less biased early version which was radicalized by the Vulgate redactor.

Had accommodation with English tradition originally been an underlying goal in the *Historia*, then I seriously doubt that the passage of dominion would have been placed where it is in the First Variant (FV, 11.7, p 254). The end of British rule falls right before Augustine's arrival, and no pre-Galfridian writer provides authority for locating this crucial juncture so late in the sixth century. The redactor of the First Variant has been forced by the contours of his source into marking the division as he does. He is seeking to reconcile a text of the *Historia* – one similar in outline to the Vulgate – with prevailing English notions on the question of periodization. In the ensuing discussion the reasons for seizing upon Augustine's mission will become clear.

Although the First Variant stands out in the manuscript transmission of the *Historia*, the redactor is not alone in what he attempts. Similar efforts at reconciliation mark the vernacular paraphrases, as well as the systematic histories, and without exception twelfth-century writers seem to be reacting to the periodization which survives in its most elaborate and most radical form in the Vulgate. This does not preclude the possibility of a pre-Vulgate recension, but it would mean that any such text closely resembled the Standard Version in contour and perspective.[47]

The present study examines the reception of Geoffrey's proposed periodization in the twelfth century. On this point writers were able to compare the *Historia* with other sources in a way that they could not do for earlier sections of Geoffrey's account. The distribution of information on early Insular history is a key factor in determining the sometimes curious usage patterns, and Chapter 1 takes up the availability of controlling data. Because the *Historia* is essentially a didactic construct, the periodization can only be understood in light of Geoffrey's intent, and Chapter 2 is devoted to an interpretive analysis of the relevant sections. Chapter 3 takes up the systematizers of history, Chapter 4 the *Brut* tradition with additional discussion of the First Variant. The investigation draws to a close around the year 1200, when the initial shockwaves generated by the appearance of the *Historia regum Britanniae* have died, and when Geoffrey has gained the stature of acknowledged authority. A considerable period of time would pass before serious controversy once again swirled about Geoffrey's depiction.

1· new light on
a shadowed past

Prior to the second quarter of the twelfth century information on pre-Saxon Britain was sparse and largely discontinuous. The deeds of the island's early Celtic inhabitants had left few traces in extant sources. Scattered entries afforded brief glimpses of isolated events, but no coherent account of British rule had survived. In fact, the period of Roman domination constituted the first discernible epoch in Insular history. For Bede and the annalists of the *Anglo-Saxon Chronicle*, the record of events began with Caesar's expeditions (HE, 1.2, pp 20–2; ASC, pp 5–6). Of the island's history before the coming of the Romans virtually nothing could be reported. The prefatory descriptions of Britain serve in lieu of a historical survey, but these sections contain mostly geographic data.[1] In the ninth century the *Historia Brittonum* added a store of legendary materials, but these did not fundamentally alter the fact that recorded history started abruptly with the events of 55–4 BC (HB, cc 7–19, pp 147–62). The principal guides to what little remained of Britain's pre-Saxon past were Latin historians with a decidedly Imperial bias.

Had Insular accounts once been available, then Gildas, a Briton by birth, might be expected to have knowledge of such records. But he too begins with Roman Britain and must rely heavily on Continental historiographers. Before surveying the course of events, Gildas comments on the source problem. Circumstance has forced him to draw not from local records, but from the 'transmarina relatione, quae crebris inrupta intercapedinibus non satis claret' (DEB, c 4, p 29). If British historical documents ever existed ('si qua fuerint'), then the texts must either have been destroyed by fire or removed by exiles.

Gildas was right to cast doubt on the existence of local historical records, if only parenthetically. His scepticism would seem based on empirical evidence, but the inference drawn, regarding the probable cause of this lamentable circumstance, misses an essential point. Gildas lived at a time when British culture remained largely pre-literate where the keeping of historical records was concerned. Prolonged contact with Roman civilization had not altered the Britons' dependence upon oral transmission for preserving noteworthy items from the past. Indeed, these traditional means would continue to be a major factor in the survival of materials bearing on Celtic history for centuries to come.

Although the lack of written British sources posed insuperable difficulties, Gildas did have access to oral traditions and drew on this repository of information. The recovery of pertinent detail from the available body of historical or quasi-historical lore would remain an integral part of the historian's craft throughout the Middle Ages. Gildas begins with events of Claudius' reign,[2] and consequently all the items presumed to be of traditional provenience bear on matters which fall after the invasion of AD 43. Pre-Roman Insular history is not included. Gildas freely admits to the selectivity of his approach and states that for didactic reasons he has passed in silence over the exploits of the valiant (DEB, c 1, p 25). Clearly Gildas knew another side to British history, but whether his information extended back into pre-Roman times is unclear. When the *Historia Brittonum* was compiled in the ninth century, no event directly involving the Britons could be assigned to the thousand-year period which separated Brutus' settlement of the island from Caesar's expeditions.[3] Gildas was familiar with Orosius and could have begun with the events of 55–4 BC had he so desired.[4] But how extensive his knowledge of earlier periods might have been remains obscure. Although many traditions current in Gildas' day probably did not survive into the ninth century, some caution would seem advisable in assessing the likely content of oral lore available to him.[5]

Whatever memories of events and personages the Britons might once have preserved, there is no indication that such oral traditions ever reached the written cultures of the non-Celtic world. The Romans perforce drew on materials which they themselves compiled, and these data would form the basis for all subsequent treatments of pre-Saxon British history by both Insular and Continental writers down to the appearance of the *Historia regum Britanniae*. As Gildas states in the passage cited above (DEB, c 4, p 29), the surviving record from across the Channel was filled with gaps. The character and distribution of the available written materials mirrored the history of Roman involvement in Insular affairs.

Except for the data on Roman Britain, classical and post-classical authors possessed very little information on the Insular Celts. Continental sources did not record a single event which antedated Caesar's expeditions. Britain had, to be sure, attracted some geographic and ethnographic interest earlier, but only of a very general nature. Little was known beyond the location of the island and the Celtic make-up of its populace.[6] Caesar hesitated to undertake military operations in Britain on the basis of such meagre information and sought to remedy the situation before crossing the Channel with his expeditionary forces. When the interrogation of Gaulish traders failed to yield sufficient specific data, Volusenus was dispatched to reconnoitre by ship.[7] Before the Roman landings Britain's isolation from recorded history was virtually complete, and even after the island had become the object of military concern, the historical background of its inhabitants remained obscure.

Down to the first century BC historians had little reason to turn their attentions to so remote an island. British affairs did not impinge upon the politics of the Mediterranean basin. For all practical purposes, the Britons generated history in a realm apart. The ramifications of events exhausted themselves within this sphere and required no systematic treatment by writers to the southeast. Toward the close of the second century BC the influx of Germanic tribes into Transalpine Gaul inaugurated an era of Roman military involvement in this relatively new province. The forces set in motion would eventually bring the legions to Britain's shores, but for many years the Belgic tribes served as a buffer between the Insular Celts and hostile interests, whether Roman or Germanic. In 57 BC, however, Caesar conquered the Belgae piecemeal, and the new threat posed by Roman control of the maritime regions prompted British intervention on the Continent of a kind which could not be ignored. The uprisings of 56 BC found Insular levies being used as reinforcements. According to Caesar, the Britons' support of the Celtic cause made invasion of the island a necessity (DBG, 4.20, p 112). A stable peace could hardly be achieved if Rome suffered the supplying of insurgents by an independent Britain. The long period of comparative isolation ended when the conduct of Insular affairs interfered with Roman aspirations.

The initial encounters between the Romans and the Britons followed a pattern which would become all too familiar in Insular history. When Britain attracted the attention of a Continental power, the island's isolation proved illusory. Caesar's expeditions produced neither lasting military results nor sustained historiographic interest. The information gathered over two successive summers of campaigning remained isolated. It was not until the Claudian Invasion inaugurated a period of Roman occupation and administration that certain kinds of data received fairly consistent notice by Continental writers. Physical presence made possible the accumulation of material on contemporary affairs, and gave at least some events immediate relevance for the Empire's historians.

With the Claudian Invasion Britain became the most northerly appurtenance of a far-flung Empire which dominated historical perceptions in late antiquity.

During the period of Roman rule several kinds of historical writing flourished on the Continent, but where remote territories were concerned, historiographers tended to view events from an Imperial perspective. Regional history was not important in its own right, a fact which severely limited the amount of detailed information recorded. The available data were evaluated and culled with an eye to their impact on Imperial politics. British history possessed no intrinsic value, and, generally speaking, only local matters which directly affected the Empire were noted. The participation of an illustrious Roman in Insular affairs might prompt the recording of somewhat greater detail, but only because his career figured prominently in Imperial history. Despite the growing importance of the historical monograph, no citizen of the Empire treated the years of dominion over Britain as a separate subject. When compared with the preceding epoch, the period of Roman dominion produced a wealth of historical materials, but of a special kind. The writers in question were not concerned with providing a comprehensive survey of provincial history, nor did they select their data from the standpoint of importance to the Britons. Consequently, the surviving material on Britain's membership in the Roman Empire could never provide a real substitute for local records.

During the Roman occupation Latin became the language of administration, major commerce, and – to an extent more difficult to determine – everyday communication between Britons.[8] Although linguistic competence certainly does not presuppose formal training, provincial schools were established in Britain and seem to have had a considerable influence.[9] There can be little doubt that at least in the lowland urban areas the process of acculturation reached a very advanced stage, accompanied by a rising literacy rate. These developments, however, do not appear to have resulted in Celtic-Latin historical writing, and some possible reasons suggest themselves. History was not taught in Roman schools, and without specific instruction even an educated Briton could hardly be expected to perceive the long-term advantages for his own culture of transmitting historical data in written form. The inherent weaknesses of oral-traditional methods become obvious only in retrospect, and only when some basis for comparison exists. I think it unlikely that substantial numbers of Britons were even familiar with this particular use of writing. No Roman historian is known to have composed his account in Britain, and in all probability none did. As a result, only the keeping of daily administrative and commercial records would have been apparent to the local populace. Detailed ethnological information is lacking for the Britons, but Continental Celtic peoples had long employed writing for specific applications, while preservation of the cultural heritage was carried on orally.[10] If the Romans were judged solely on the basis of the observable uses of writing, then a similar division might reasonably have been postulated for them. Be that as it may, Insular historiographic activity was not one of the immediate by-products of Romanization.

Data bearing on many aspects of contemporary Insular history were gathered by the Romans in the normal course of provincial administration. Official records and personal observations greatly increased the store of available knowledge, but the writing of history took place far from Britain's shores. Information flowed from this remote province toward the centre of the Empire, and quite probably both the quantity and the quality of the data suffered as a result. Despite the problems inherent in purveying the materials of history across any considerable distance, events would prove that the point of greatest vulnerability lay at the source. The acquisition of Insular data for use in historical writing depended upon the Roman presence. When the legions departed and the administration collapsed, information was cut off at the point of origin.

In the fifth century, Roman writers found much to occupy their attention and paid little heed to a distant former province. Contemporary or near-contemporary references to Insular occurrences became exceedingly rare on the Continent, while the Britons themselves still kept no written historical records. In Gaul writers did note some items bearing on Insular history, but not to the extent which might have been expected. During the fourth and fifth centuries the intellectual contacts between Britain and Gaul seem to have been fairly extensive.[11] Yet despite the documented travels of British churchmen and the presumed transit of British pilgrims, the information in Gaulish sources remains disappointingly meagre.[12] Bede did, to be sure, draw on Prosper Tiro's *Epitoma chronicon* and Constantius' *Vita Germani*. But where fifth-century Insular history is concerned, the information culled from these two works bears only on the career of St Germanus.

During the first half of the fifth century the teachings of the British heresiarch Pelagius attracted the attention of Western Christendom's leading churchmen. When Pelagianism continued to flourish in Britain, Prosper reports that Celestine, the bishop of Rome, asked Germanus' help in suppressing this heretical doctrine.[13] The bishop of Auxerre is said to have visited Britain in 429, but Prosper seems poorly informed as to what actually transpired on the other side of the Channel.[14] He knows nothing of a second visit, nor does he note the advent of Anglo-Saxon rule. By the middle of the century, however, Prosper Tiro had moved from Gaul, and it is distinctly possible that news of Insular developments simply failed to reach him.[15] Constantius does provide a fairly full account of Germanus' activities in Britain, but there is a notable absence of detail.[16] None of the incidents recounted is assigned to a specific locale and date.

Hagiographers exhibit a notorious lack of concern for chronological precision; indeed, most of the miracles reported by Constantius can be found with minor variations in countless other saints' lives. Only the Alleluia Victory has the feel of an event with some basis in historical fact.[17]

The sequence of events leading to written notice of Germanus' Insular career reveals a great deal about the concerns of Continental authors in the fifth century. Pelagius probably arrived in Rome not long after the year 400. Nothing is known of his background or of his earlier activities; indeed, had he not spread heretical teachings on the Continent, Pelagius might have left no trace. Prosper remarks that Celestine was the first bishop of Rome to take an active interest in Insular affairs.[18] The statement may not be completely accurate, but certainly within living memory Britain had never attracted such interest.[19] The controversy ignited by Pelagius on the Continent drew the attention of Celestine and others to the island which had spawned this heresiarch. The discovery that Pelagianism flourished in Britain prompted the request to Germanus. If allowed to go unchecked, there would be nothing to prevent a steady stream of heretics from spreading a doctrine which struck at the very heart of Roman orthodoxy. Germanus intervened in Insular affairs to protect the interests of the Continental Church. His visit to Britain attracted written notice because Pelagianism was a matter of major concern to the Continent. What governed the selection of data in fifth-century Gaul was exactly the same standard of relevance which underlay the materials included by earlier, more secularly minded Roman historians.

The inference drawn from Prosper and Constantius receives confirmation from the other two writers who provide near-contemporary testimony on fifth-century Britain. Zosimus, probably quoting Olympiodorus, reports that under the usurper Magnus Maximus the Britons seceded from the Roman Empire and were forced to defend themselves against foreign incursion.[20] Procopius describes a practice brought about by the rapid population growth of the Frisians and the Anglo-Saxons in Britain. Every year large numbers of people are said to have been sent to the Franks, who provided Continental lands for settlement.[21] The accuracy of Procopius' account is not at issue, any more than the historicity of incidents reported by Constantius. Important is the pattern of inclusions: only items which bear in some way on Britain's relationship to the Continent receive notice.

How widespread knowledge of the Germanic invasions may have been is difficult to say. The Anglo-Saxon ascendancy did not affect Continental policy-making, and for the most part contemporary historians seem to have regarded the governance of the island as a matter of strictly internal interest. On the other hand, the struggle for control of Britain would tend to militate against the transmission of detailed information across the Channel. The landings by Germanic tribesmen took place along the coastline facing Gaul, and these incursions must have affected normal intercourse. Despite the evidence of strong traditional ties between Britain and Gaul, the records for the fifth century are notoriously spotty, and the gaps could easily conceal a major interruption in Channel traffic. Be that as it may, the Britons and the Anglo-Saxons were far too absorbed in their own struggles to provide the kind of stimulus which would have attracted notice by Continental historiographers. During the fifth century Insular affairs seem to constitute essentially a closed system.

The advent of Anglo-Saxon rule did not fundamentally alter Continental attitudes toward Britain's history. Bede became well known on the other side of the Channel, and the spread of his works provided a considerable store of previously unknown materials. From the second half of the eighth century onwards Continental writers were much better informed regarding Insular affairs, but this produced no significant advances in the depiction of British and early English history. The greater availability of data prompted neither detailed consideration of Britain's past nor interest in current developments. Bede's principal importance for the history of Continental historiography lay in his system of chronology.[22] Writers did, to be sure, mine the chronicles appended to his computistical tracts, and the *Historia ecclesiastica* also enjoyed wide circulation. Such statistics must be interpreted with care. Historians on the Continent included only a small amount of the material bearing specifically on Insular affairs, and these data are reported from a perspective quite unlike Bede's.[23]

One feature of eighth- and ninth-century Continental depictions does merit discussion. Among the materials regularly selected for use was Bede's account of the barbarian incursions which plagued sub-Roman Britain, culminating in the Anglo-Saxon conquest. Unlike Gildas and Bede, Continental writers placed these events in the larger context of the Germanic migrations and the fall of the Roman Empire.[24] The Insular data provided a useful addendum to what were already regarded as developments crucial to an understanding of the fifth and sixth centuries. English writers doubtless would have benefited from this broader perspective, but the Carolingian histories in question do not appear to have exerted any influence across the Channel, whether direct or indirect. Even in the twelfth century, when compendious surveys formed such a large part of the contemporary historiographic activity, writers in England turned to much earlier sources for their information on the Empire.

Carolingian historians exhibit complete disinterest in recent Anglo-Saxon developments. Their attitude is rather surprising, given the prominence of

Englishmen in the Kingdom of the Franks during the eighth and ninth centuries. Boniface, of course, receives historiographic notice for his contribution to the spread of the faith on the Continent, but neither such missionary work nor the scholarly activity of Alcuin and others draws attention to the history of the island whence these men came. Carolingian writers treat them as Continental figures whose accomplishments can be understood without reference to Insular developments.[25] To judge from the silence of the *Anglo-Saxon Chronicle*, English annalists also regarded men like Boniface and Alcuin as important only to the Continent.[26] The extraordinarily heavy cross-Channel traffic between centres of learning left few historiographic traces,[27] but other types of evidence, particularly the surviving letters, attest to how well-informed at least the leading figures of the day actually were.

The history of relations between England and the Continent during the Carolingian era simply cannot be written from contemporary chronicles. Indeed, down to the Norman Conquest it would be well-nigh impossible to distinguish periods of Anglo-Saxon influence from periods of comparative isolation using only historiographic witnesses. On the basis of the data supplied, one might be tempted to conclude that England's relationship to the Continent was the same during the reign of Charlemagne, as it was at the height of the Danish invasions, when the forces of history actually threatened for a time to sunder the island's ties with non-Scandinavian Europe. Chronicle entries on both sides of the Channel bespeak the fairly rigorous exclusion of information which did not bear directly on regional developments, whether temporal or ecclesiastical. In many cases the Continental perspective was significantly broader than the Insular, but, generally speaking, writers took notice only when one history impinged upon the other. The Battle of Hastings was just such a juncture, and by the twelfth century its aftermath had brought about significant changes in the prevailing attitudes toward Britain's past.

The Norman Conquest drew England into the mainstream of European politics to an extent unparalleled since the Claudian Invasion over a millennium earlier.[28] As part of a steadily expanding Norman domain, the island assumed a new importance for the balance of power on the Continent. William's successors were not always able to style themselves both Duke of Normandy and King of England, but the impact on historical perceptions was great nonetheless. Just as the Britons once regarded themselves as citizens of Rome, so now the island's inhabitants saw themselves and their history in a European context, a view shared at least in some Continental circles. Unlike the Roman period, when the Britons kept no historical records of their own, the historiographic response to the Norman Conquest must be traced on both sides of the Channel.

Although few Continental writers pass in silence over Hastings, physical proximity and perceptions of historical relevance continue to govern the selection of data. The level of interest in Anglo-Norman affairs, as reflected in the number of entries, tends to decrease with geographic remove. Historians in traditionally Imperial lands betray a decidedly Mediterranean orientation and do not report developments to the northwest with any consistency.[29] This distribution pattern is important for an understanding of where historiographic interest in Britain's past first manifests itself on the Continent following the Norman Conquest.

Within a half-century of Hastings, Sigebert of Gembloux provides a clear indication of the change in Continental attitudes. His universal chronicle continued the work of Eusebius and Jerome, but Sigebert numbered the Insular peoples among those whose histories merited tracing down through the ages.[30] There can be little doubt that his view of the contemporary balance of political power prompted this decision. In Jerome's day the inclusion of a separate column for the kings of Britain had not seemed warranted,[31] but after centuries of comparative neglect on the part of Continental writers the Norman Conquest sparked new interest in the contours of Insular history. The significance of Hastings made some consideration of the background essential, but Sigebert did not stop with the succession problems following the death of Edward the Confessor, as so many did. Within the limits of the available sources Sigebert extended this line of historical inquiry back across the entire time-span covered by his depiction, producing the first systematic consideration of Insular history by a Continental writer.[32]

Throughout the twelfth century Sigebert of Gembloux served as an important link between the large-scale survey of Continental tradition and historiographic developments in the Anglo-Norman domain. By incorporating Britain's past into the framework of universal history, Sigebert ensured that his chronicle would be used by English and Norman writers who sought to place Insular developments in a larger context. Sigebert's work was supplemented and continued by numerous historians during the twelfth century.

Like the Carolingian writers before him, Sigebert knew only Bede's *Chronica majora* and *Historia ecclesiastica*. A much higher percentage of the Insular data found in these works was included by him, but he could not move beyond his sources for the earliest periods. As a direct result of Sigebert's total dependence on Bede, pre-Saxon British history remained essentially a blank. Furthermore, Sigebert seriously distorted the already compressed chronology of Bede's depiction of the fifth and sixth centuries. A single annal encompasses the events from Germanus' first visit through the Battle of Mount Badon (sg, a 446, p 309).[33] In England a highly differentiated picture of at least the Germanic take-over was available in the *Anglo-Saxon Chronicle*, but the language of composition undoubtedly precluded use of this source by Continental historians. Certainly there is no evidence of its dissemination on the other side of the Channel in Sigebert's day.[34]

Advances in the depiction of early Insular history had to come from England. A Continental writer with Sigebert's interests could do little but content himself with Bede while awaiting further historiographic developments. In the second and third decades of the twelfth century Insular historians set to work systematizing the available data with an eye toward producing a comprehensive overview in Latin. William of Malmesbury took the first step in this direction and established what was to become the prevalent pattern in the use of English sources. The *Anglo-Saxon Chronicle* provided William with the underlying chronological framework, and supplementary materials from Bede were then intercalated to produce a coherent account.

The *Worcester Chronicle* exhibits the same combination, even though the compilation process was rather different. The Worcester chronicler began with Marianus Scotus, thereby providing evidence of the importance of Continental models for what Insular writers sought to accomplish. Unlike Sigebert, Marianus was primarily concerned with problems of chronology, but his scant treatment of Britain's past did derive from Bede.[35] At Worcester the *Anglo-Saxon Chronicle* was interpolated into Marianus' framework. Although additional material from Bede does not appear to have been added, the two constituent elements in the depiction of early English history remain essentially the same as in William's *Gesta regum Anglorum*.

By whatever means, the combining of Bede with the *Anglo-Saxon Chronicle* resulted in the virtual exclusion of the Britons from any consideration. Neither William of Malmesbury nor the Worcester chronicler has anything of substance to report on the Insular Celts. The omission, however, is not as noticeable as might be expected. William expressly limits himself to English history and seems to have considered the Britons a negligible force after the first Saxon landing. In the *Worcester Chronicle* the much broader scope of the depiction tends to obscure the loss of the entire pre-Saxon era. The account sketches the familiar contours of universal history, and in the absence of evidence to suggest the Britons' importance for an understanding of the standard paradigms, their omission would attract little attention. No attempt was made either in the *Gesta regum Anglorum* or in the *Worcester Chronicle* to incorporate British history into the overview. Henry of Huntingdon's *Historia Anglorum* marked the first effort in this direction, but when the pre-Saxon materials were assembled, the paucity of data became painfully evident. The problem with the available information emerged only when serious consideration was given to the Britons. Henry's depiction of British history was seriously limited by both the quantity and coherence of the material.[36]

The composition of the pre-Saxon segment of the *Historia Anglorum* (Book 1) antedates Henry's first glimpse of the *Historia regum Britanniae* at Bec in 1139.[37] Subsequent revisions were made, including minor additions from Geoffrey, but the depiction remained essentially pre-Galfridian.[38] For Henry, as for his predecessors, the systematic portion of the account could begin only with Caesar (HA, 1.12, p 16). Even after the first recorded contacts with Rome, the dearth of Insular materials necessitated heavy reliance on what were ultimately Roman sources. Indeed, from the arrival of Caesar's expeditionary forces (55 BC) through the Britons' appeal to Aetius (446–50 AD) Henry employs the Roman succession as the only viable framework for a chronology (HA, 1.12–46, pp 16–35). Much of the data bears more directly on Imperial politics than on Insular concerns, but Henry could do little else. A well-structured account was possible only from a Roman perspective. With the departure of the legions came total dependence on local materials and a concomitant loss in clarity of outline. The situation improved gradually after the arrival of Hengist and Horsa, because from this point forward Henry was able to combine Bede with the *Anglo-Saxon Chronicle* to produce a coherent, if not always detailed account.

Henry's skilful handling of the Roman materials obfuscated some difficulties, but certainly not all. As Warin the Briton was quick to point out, the combination of available sources actually underscored the existence of a major lacuna. Henry's epistolary summary of the *Historia regum Britanniae* came in response to Warin's question regarding this gap: 'Quæris a me, Warine Brito, vir comis et facete, cur patriæ nostræ gesta narrans, a temporibus Julii Cæsaris inceperim, et florentissima regna, quæ a Bruto usque ad Julium fuerunt, omiserim.'[39]

Warin had perceived what was a major weakness in the *Historia Anglorum*. Following a preliminary descriptive section (HA, 1.1–8, pp 5–13), Henry took up the settlement of Britain and recounted the story of Brutus from the *Historia Brittonum* (HA, 1.9, p 13; HB, c 10, pp 149–53). The reign of this eponymous hero was dated by means of a synchronism which derived from the same source: 'Dicunt autem illi auctores, quod quando Bruto regnabat in Britannia, Hely sacerdos judicabat in Israel, et Posthumus sive Silvius filius Æneæ regnabat apud Latinos, cujus nepos erat Bruto' (HA, 1.9, p 13; cf HB, c 11, p 153). The origins of the Irish and the Picts were then discussed, before Henry turned to Julius Caesar.[40] Between Eli's judgeship (c 1100 BC) and Caesar's expeditions (55–4 BC) lay more than a thousand years; yet not a single historical occurrence was assigned to this period. By way of explanation Henry described his fruitless search for information: 'Respondeo igitur tibi quod nec voce nec scripto horum temporum sæpissime notitiam quærens invenire potui' (RT, 1:97). Now, to his amazement, he had found a work which filled the lacuna.

The distribution of materials on early Insular history has long been seen as a key factor in the success of Geoffrey's imaginative depiction. A medieval historian's ability to render critical judgments on the reliability of his sources is a function of the availability of data. Only in cases where a basis for comparison exists, can a writer exercise some modicum of control. Geoffrey of Monmouth undoubtedly traded on this fact. That his stunning achievement represented a gross violation and wilful manipulation of accepted historiographic practice was often suspected, but difficult to prove. The extent to which his account overlaps with standard authorities is exceedingly small. Geoffrey is the only source for most of what he reports. Even when he treats well-attested matters, Geoffrey of Monmouth offers a British point of view not to be found elsewhere. His approach is seemingly orthodox, the events endowed with surpassing verisimilitude. In the absence of controlling data it was inordinately difficult to catch him in a lie.

Medieval historiographers lacked reliable means for determining what should and should not become part of the canon of history. For the distant past the historicity of the preponderance of data was established by simple reference to authority. Information concerning remote eras had passed through the hands of men whose veracity was not open to question. The odd crux might remain, but a pre-selection process operated which largely obviated the necessity for critical judgments. This method of evaluating data from the distant past proved vulnerable long before Geoffrey of Monmouth. Erroneous and pseudonymous attributions were commonplace in the Middle Ages, and Geoffrey most assuredly did not invent the old-book topos. Indeed, the *Historia* was pseudo-history of a kind found in every medieval founding story. For the most part, such historical fictions could not be sustained over any considerable time-span. Geoffrey's *Historia* differed from other examples in scope and skill of execution, but not in underlying assumption. Scores of writers, both before and after, exploited the same weakness in the methods employed for screening historical data. The age placed great stock in authority, because the means of verification were so limited. The likelihood that a specific item could be and would be compared with a putative source was exceedingly small. The very practices instituted to guarantee accuracy provided the favourite devices for justifying the spurious.

The physical location of writers and sources remained an important consideration throughout the Middle Ages. Generally speaking, monastic chroniclers found themselves limited to materials available in a relatively small geographic area. Religious communities situated close to courts or along pilgrimage routes enjoyed a natural advantage over more isolated monasteries. A few writers were able to travel extensively in conjunction with their offices, thereby gaining wider access to sources of information. But even for individuals fortunate enough to undertake such journeys, chance encounter played a significant role. Henry of Huntingdon discovered the *Historia regum Britanniae* at Bec; yet Geoffrey resided in the diocese of Lincoln, where Henry was an archdeacon.[41] The willingness to believe that certain materials survived in a rare, even unique copy of a work, available only to another writer, was not merely a sign of credulousness. The historiographic holdings of medieval libraries varied enormously, and chroniclers could not hope to check every entry of their predecessors or contemporaries. Trust in an author's veracity might turn out to be misplaced, but some measure of reliance on the testimony of others was absolutely unavoidable.

Geoffrey wrote in an age when early Insular history was still being given shape. Efforts to produce a coherent overview of the island's past dominated contemporary historiography. For William of Malmesbury, the Worcester chronicler, and Henry of Huntingdon, the systematization of history was not motivated by a sudden infusion of new data. Each writer endeavoured to impose order on a store of information which had gone largely unchanged for centuries. Not only had the size of the corpus remained static, but earlier attempts to systematize the data were few in number. Since the passing of Bede, only Æthelweard had undertaken the task, and William of Malmesbury found much to criticize in the style of this late tenth-century chronicle.[42] Writers regarded the materials of Insular history as essentially unordered; yet the *Anglo-Saxon Chronicle* provided a chronological framework for a major segment of the past. At issue was the use of the available information to delineate major developments and, by so doing, to identify the forces which had shaped Insular history. Systematizers in the first half of the twelfth century perceived a need to render the course of events comprehensible. The order sought by these men went beyond the chronological arrangement of data to the interpretation of history.

In addition to the uneven distribution of materials, two major obstacles impeded the progress toward a coherent overview. The first was Britain's long, disjunctive history. The welter of events, punctuated by foreign incursion, largely exceeded human understanding. For this reason the view was widely held that the many vicissitudes constituted divine retribution visited on a sinful populace. The difficulties inherent in the data were compounded by the almost total lack of historiographic conventions bearing specifically on the shape of Britain's history. No patterning devices had evolved from which writers in the twelfth century might extrapolate. For Bede the progress of the apostolic faith served as a unifying principle, especially in the early sections of the account. But the further he moved from Augustine's mission, the more difficult it became to organize the material around this single thread. The loose structure of the closing books in the *Historia ecclesiastica* bears witness to the problem. Æthelweard's attempt to impute universal significance to Anglo-Saxon history resulted only in a gross disparity between the frame and the data. He lacked an effective contact point with the larger structures of history, and therefore could not tap the dynamism of the standard paradigms. Given both the character of Insular history and the dearth of conventions, it is hardly surprising that the efforts to systematize the materials fell far short of consistent interpretation.

Despite the difficulties, the first decades of the twelfth century witnessed considerable progress, at least where the Anglo-Saxon and Norman periods were concerned. Writers drew on a comparatively small number of sources and quickly approached consensus on the outlines, if not on matters of interpretation. The first substantial block of new data to require incorporation into this emerging overview was the *Historia regum Britanniae*. Geoffrey filled the notorious pre-Saxon lacuna with an essentially discrete block of history. The account treated the period from the settlement of the island to the passing of British rule. Although Merlin's prophecies spanned the later epochs, no attempt was made to depict the subsequent course of events in systematic fashion. Geoffrey presupposed the historiographic activity of his own day, a fact which would seem to be confirmed by the epilogue to the *Historia*. Here it is stated that anyone interested in the kings who reigned after the close of the seventh century should consult Caradog of Llancarfan for Wales and William of Malmesbury or Henry of Huntingdon for England.[43] Geoffrey's contemporaries and near-contemporaries had obviated the necessity of extending the account to include more recent history, be it Welsh or Anglo-Saxon.

Although Geoffrey depicted a discrete and largely unknown segment of Insular history, he clearly regarded his account as compatible with the prevailing view of subsequent events. Were this not the case, Geoffrey of Monmouth could hardly have relied on Merlin's prophecies to bridge the chronological gap between the end of the *Historia* and twelfth-century England. The vatic utterances evoked what he correctly presumed to be familiar historical contours.[44] Merlin offered a preview which agreed in general outline with the accounts of Geoffrey's contemporaries. The seer did what no medieval chronicler could do before, namely he surveyed the entire course of Britain's history from a consistently Insular perspective. The series of prophecies reveals a highly significant advantage which accrued to historiographers using the *Historia regum Britanniae*. Geoffrey's account permitted a continuity of viewpoint which transcended the interruptions produced by foreign invasion.

Despite the usefulness and seeming orthodoxy of the *Historia*, twelfth-century historiographers exhibit considerable ambivalence toward this new source. After centuries of ignorance regarding pre-Saxon history, the very brilliance of Geoffrey's depiction elicited caution. To discover so much material for so distant an era was unusual. That anecdotes and other minor items might have escaped the notice of earlier writers was plausible, even expected, but the timely recovery of an entire age struck contemporaries as less likely. On the other hand, the existence of such a huge lacuna was itself puzzling. Continental sources for the period in question left much to be desired, but the record of events was significantly better than the Insular survivals. The twelfth century saw no obvious reason for this discrepancy, and the difficulties inherent in historical research only compounded the uncertainty. It must be assumed that Henry of Huntingdon embarked upon his search for pre-Saxon materials in the very real hope of finding additional information.[45] The early history of more than one people owed its survival to chance preservation in a single source.

Historians responded to Geoffrey's depiction by scouring standard authorities for corroborating testimony. Some supporting evidence was deemed necessary for an account which so radically altered the prevailing view of the Britons. Geoffrey of Monmouth, however, insinuated his portrayal into the numerous gaps left by previous writers. He seemed to anticipate the response of his contemporaries and successfully avoided factual contradictions throughout much of the *Historia*. Although Geoffrey displayed extraordinary skill, difficulties did occur. The problems in the post-Arthurian segment differed substantially from those in earlier portions of the text. The two sections must be kept separate in any discussion of the factors influencing Geoffrey's reception.

Down to the reign of Arthur, the *Historia regum Britanniae* agreed in general outline with what little could be surmised regarding the shape of British history. This framework imposed few restrictions on Geoffrey; indeed, there was no surviving record of Insular occurrence for the millennium which separated Brutus from Cassibellaunus. Geoffrey supplied a regnal list for the pre-Roman era and far beyond, interspersing brief characterizations with rather lengthy royal biographies.[46] In his account the Britons emerged as a people with a rich past, one filled with examples of human greatness and human folly.

So far as Geoffrey and his contemporaries were concerned, only Rome boasted a coherent record of events for the period in question. Britain's early isolation had long been proverbial, and local occurrences would hardly be expected to attract the notice of historians in the Mediterranean basin. Consequently, Geoffrey of Monmouth enjoyed complete freedom in depicting matters of strictly Insular concern. Care had to be taken only with points of contact between British and Roman history. Geoffrey appears fully cognizant of this limitation. It is surely not by accident that Brutus demonstrates his worth far from the environs of Rome (HRB, cc 6–20, pp 73–90). On the other hand, Britain's eponym is the great-grandson of Aeneas, and can be seen retracing the peregrinations of his illustrious ancestor. Geoffrey even elaborates the parallels with extensive borrowings from Virgil.[47] Roman historiography might represent the sole potential control on the depiction, but the City's past also possessed paradigmatic value.

Rome serves as the standard against which British achievement is measured. Geoffrey's depiction of the Britons' early potential does not hinge solely on Brutus' ancestry. The founding story gives impetus to the narration, but the thrust would quickly dissipate without comparison of a more direct kind. Geoffrey gauges the Britons' strengths and weaknesses through military encounters with Rome. The standard authorities record no such armed conflicts prior to Caesar's expeditions, but the *Historia* offers a different picture. During the post-settlement period the Britons demonstrate a capacity for real greatness and actually conquer Rome over three centuries before Caesar's arrival. The care taken in handling this episode attests to Geoffrey's awareness that Roman historiography provided the only check on the early sections of the *Historia*.

The conquest of Rome is attributed to the leadership of Belinus and Brennius. Acting in concert, the two brothers defeat first the Gauls and then the Romans (HRB, cc 42–4, pp 115–18).[48] Belinus returns to Britain after the fall of the City and rules in peace for the rest of his life. Brennius remains in Italy, where he treats the populace with extreme severity. Geoffrey characterizes Brennius' subsequent career only briefly. The interested reader is invited to consult Roman histories for additional information: 'Habita ergo victoria, remansit Brennius in Italia, populum inaudita tyrannide afficiens. Cujus ceteros actus et exitum, quia romanae historiae declarant, nequaquam tractare curavi, cum et nimiam prolixitatem huic operi ingessissem et, id quod alii tractaverunt perarans, a proposito meo divertissem' (HRB, c 44, p 118). This statement follows a familiar pattern, but further research would indeed yield more data. Geoffrey has appropriated Brennus, commander of the Senonian Gauls who sacked Rome in 390 BC.[49] A Continental Celt has been transformed into a Briton, but Geoffrey knew full well that the background of the historical Brennus was obscure. Rather than serving as a control, the Roman testimony actually seemed to confirm Geoffrey's account.[50]

This pattern of usage recurs in the depiction of Caesar's invasions and throughout the sections dealing with the period of Roman domination. Whenever possible, Geoffrey employs well-attested matters to lend credence to the account. Through the addition of countless details, familiar events are recounted from a decidedly Insular perspective, but the basic elements admit of ready corroboration. Previous accounts contained little more than a sparse outline, making refutation of Geoffrey's depiction inordinately difficult. The twelfth century simply could not adduce any hard evidence to the contrary. There was only the silence of standard authorities to gainsay the level of attainment depicted in the *Historia*. For writers accustomed to relying on Continental sources for their knowledge concerning Roman Britain, the omission of so much material did raise questions. The character of the corroborating testimony was merely puzzling for the early sections, but a major problem for the reign of Arthur.

The first man to comment on the absence of supporting evidence is Alfred of Beverley.[51] Approximately half of his modest and highly derivative history is given over to a depiction of British rule. Geoffrey's regnal list provides the underlying framework, but Alfred is openly distrustful of his principal source. Four criteria are cited as forming a basis for the selection of data from the *Historia*. Alfred promises to recount only such matters as 1/ are credible, 2/ make good reading, 3/ will stick in readers' minds, and 4/ can be corroborated by the testimony of other authorities (AB, pp 2–3). These criteria apply exclusively to the selection of data from Geoffrey's account. Alfred of Beverley did not apply the four tests with any rigour, nor could he.[52] But the practicability of such a selection process does not alter the fact that Alfred perceived a need to establish the scrupulousness with which the *Historia regum Britanniae* had been handled. He remarks the lack of corroboration on two occasions, but only after he has included the materials in question.

Book 1 of the *Annales* treats the lengthy period of independent British rule from Brutus through Lud (AB, pp 10–23).[53] At the start of Book 2 Alfred describes how he scoured Pompeius Trogus, Suetonius, Eutropius, and Orosius for some mention of the sovereigns who so dominate the first epoch in Britain's history. Gildas and Bede were also consulted (AB, p 24). This extensive research failed to yield information on the British monarchs who ruled prior to Caesar's arrival. Despite the care taken by Geoffrey, Alfred apparently did not identify Brennius with Brennus the Gaul.[54] No further comment is offered, but what prompted the observation can perhaps be inferred. Alfred is about to depict the centuries of Roman domination, a period for which there is a comparative abundance of supporting data. The account in fact ceases to be an epitome of the *Historia* and becomes a compilation of familiar sources, including Geoffrey. It is the contrast with the preceding epoch which has elicited the comment. Alfred signals a change in the availability of corroborating testimony, but he does not call attention to any particular problems raised by the distribution of data.

In the second instance Alfred is more explicit. At the close of his depiction of British history he wonders aloud that 'de inclito rege Arturo nichil Romana, nichil Anglorum hystoria meminerit, cum tamen ipse non solum in Britannia contra paganos, sed et in Galliis contra Romanos res præclaras ingenii audacia miraque probitate gesserit' (AB, p 76). Alfred follows Geoffrey closely in depicting King Arthur's career (AB, pp 58–73). The fabled sovereign rules over a far-flung domain and even challenges the authority of Rome. Indeed, Arthur doubtless would have triumphed, had he not been betrayed at home. That Continental exploits of this magnitude should have left no trace in other sources is disquieting. The gaps in Insular accounts were notorious, but Alfred apparently regarded the situation on the other side of the Channel as sufficiently better for the period in question to make Arthur's omission problematic.

Although clearly troubled, Alfred has not felt that the lack of supporting evidence warranted complete rejection of Geoffrey's account. The circumstances have, however, affected Alfred's ability to deal critically with Arthur's exploits: 'Quas [res] ego hystoricæ fidei derogare non audens, studio brevitatis ista de Britonum hystoria excerpere curavi, ut quæ incredebilia a quibusdam viderentur prætermitterem, et tamen virtuti nichil detraherem' (AB, p 76). What applies in the case of King Arthur also holds true for the rest of British history: without a second source which treats the same events, Alfred has no effective basis for rendering critical judgments on the accuracy of Geoffrey's account.

Alfred of Beverley inserted a substantial portion of Geoffrey's account into what was essentially a historical vacuum. The problems were rather different when the data had to be interpolated into a pre-existent frame. A case in point is Robert of Torigni, who grappled with the problems attendant upon incorporating materials from the *Historia regum Britanniae* into the universal chronicle of Sigebert of Gembloux.[55]

Geoffrey of Monmouth's account is notable for its remove from the standard paradigms of Christian history.[56] Robert's undertaking, however, did not entail the imposition of a schema on the data. Sigebert had continued the work of Eusebius and Jerome. Like his illustrious predecessors, Sigebert had correlated a series of essentially discrete chronologies. Such activity was an expression of belief in an underlying providential design, but did not involve the patterning of material. Sigebert's information on the Britons, the Anglo-Saxons, and the Normans was sketchy (RT, 1:94). Robert planned to interpolate data not known to Sigebert and then to continue the universal chronicle from the year 1100 (RT, 1:96). To include the *Historia regum Britanniae* would have necessitated only inserting notice of British rulers and important events into the entry for the appropriate year. Dating problems were, of course, inevitable, but Geoffrey did employ a system of synchronisms which could have facilitated the positioning of blocks of material, if not always the fixing of specific items.[57] Yet Robert of Torigni did not handle Geoffrey's account as he did other sources.

The material contained in the *Historia regum Britanniae* posed a special problem which Robert discusses in the prologue to his work. Some of the events recounted by Geoffrey were of great antiquity; indeed, Brutus was the great-grandson of Aeneas. If Robert were to include Geoffrey's entire regnal list, the names of British sovereigns would have to be interpolated not only into Sigebert's frame, but into the chronologies of Jerome and even Eusebius: 'Sed quia Brutus pronepos Æneæ, a quo et insula Britannia vocata est, primus ibi regnavit, si vellem omnes reges sibi succedentes ordine congruo ponere, necesse esset michi non solum per librum Sigisberti, verum etiam per totum corpus chronicorum Jeronimi, et per magnam partem chronographiæ Eusebii, eadem nomina spargere' (RT, 1:95–6). Robert is loath to intercalate the chronological framework of the *Historia regum Britanniae*. He regards as unseemly (*indecens*) the interpolation of outside data into the writings of men of such authority as Eusebius and Jerome (RT, 1:96). To satisfy the interested reader, he has included Henry of Huntingdon's letter to Warin (RT, 1:97–111).

That Robert of Torigni should voice his respect for Eusebius and Jerome is hardly surprising. The combined efforts of the two Fathers formed the chrono-logical basis for the writing of universal history in medieval Christendom. Robert viewed his own work in the context of this historiographic tradition, as had Sigebert before him. Sigebert of Gembloux may have added Insular history to the framework, but he had not extended the line back through the time period covered by Eusebius and Jerome. The last event reported by Jerome is the death of Valens in 378. Sigebert begins his compilation with the year 381, 'quo anno post mortem Valentis Valentinianus minor et Gratianus, filii maioris Valentiniani, incipientes simul regnare, regnaverunt annis 6' (SG, p 302). The choice of this starting point obviously depends upon Jerome, and Robert's reverence would also seem highly conventional.

Robert of Torigni's chronicle is found in manuscripts together with both Eusebius-Jerome and Sigebert [58] An examination of the interpolations made by Robert for the period before 1100 reveals a discrepancy between his avowed respect for the inviolability of Eusebius-Jerome and his actual practice. Although few in number and rather inconsequential, he did add materials bearing on events prior to 381.[59] It would seem reasonable to conclude that Robert of Torigni harboured misgivings about the *Historia* which go beyond the posturing of the prologue. I am persuaded, however, that his comments do hold the key to the handling of Geoffrey's account, and that even the interpola-tions made in Eusebius-Jerome are important for an understanding of Robert's attitude.

In discussing the *Historia regum Britanniae*, Robert of Torigni alludes both to the antiquity of events and to the large number of British kings. Although the first point raises the entire question of Eusebius and Jerome, I believe that the second touches the area of real concern. Robert's comments betray uneasiness over the quantitative impact of Geoffrey's account, and these fears can hardly be considered unjustified. In the second half of the twelfth century the situation with regard to the availability of data on the Britons differed dramatically from what it had been in Sigebert's day. Given his dependence on Bede, Robert's predecessor could have known little more than the name of Cassibellaunus for the period before 381, and the effect of interpolating such meagre data into Eusebius-Jerome would have been negligible. Robert, on the other hand, had an enormous amount of information at his disposal, so much that the deeds of the Britons might eclipse the accomplishments of other ancient peoples at least at scattered junctures. Geoffrey had succeeded in rectifying the earlier quantitative imbalance, but by so doing he had created a new problem.

Underlying the selection of material for any universal chronicle is the assumption that peoples should receive notice in proportion to their importance for the larger structures of history. Specific choices frequently reflect other factors, including a desire on the part of the writer to force reassessment of a regional history within the universal framework.[60] Such propagandistic motives notwithstanding, a correlation can be said to exist between perceived historical significance and the quantity of data supplied. To interpolate Geoffrey's entire regnal list, together with some indication of key events, would have substantially altered prevailing notions of the relative importance of peoples in antiquity, and Robert appears troubled by the implications. He never intended to undertake a major revision of traditional views as reflected in Eusebius-Jerome. That would seem to be the sense of his comments in the prologue, and the few minor interpolations made for events prior to 381 are not inconsistent with this approach. Indeed, the additions can be seen as reflecting Robert's conception of what constitutes the extent of change permissible in the work of two such venerable authorities.

Robert's attitude toward Sigebert was entirely different, but this fact did not have practical consequences for the handling of Geoffrey's *Historia*. Sigebert of Gembloux had begun his chronicle with the joint rule of Valentinianus and Gratianus, but lacked much of the material available to Robert on Insular and Norman history. Robert of Torigni systematically went back over the centuries treated by Sigebert, adding data previously unknown outside a small geographic area. The number of interpolations increases steadily, as Robert approaches the twelfth century, and he takes over the account completely with the annal for 1100. It was Sigebert, not Eusebius and Jerome, who incorporated Insular history into the universal chronicle, and Robert of Torigni exhibits no reluctance to interpolate substantial amounts of material on Britain's past into Sigebert's frame. Geoffrey of Monmouth also notes the accession of

Valentinianus and Gratianus (HRB, c 80, p 154). Beginning at this point, Robert could have picked up Geoffrey's account without any significant change in his handling of Sigebert; in fact the *Historia* would seem to offer precisely the kind of supplementary data required. Between 381 and Cadwaladr's death in 689 lay over three centuries of British history, including the reign of Arthur. Robert made numerous additions to Sigebert for the period in question; yet none came from the *Historia regum Britanniae*.[61] It is difficult to know what importance should be attached to the exclusion of Galfridian materials for the years from 381 to 689. By Robert's day the *Historia* had gained such popularity that to include only the latter part of Geoffrey's account might have raised more problems than it solved. I am inclined to think that such restricted usage probably was not a real possibility.

Robert of Torigni clearly regarded any effort to incorporate the early sections of Geoffrey's *Historia* into Eusebius-Jerome as inherently problematic. His hesitancy would seem to stem from the quantitative impact of the Galfridian materials on traditional conceptions of history, and I think that more cannot be read into the evidence. Robert voices no distrust of Geoffrey's factual accuracy and includes the whole of Henry of Huntingdon's epistolary summary without caveat. The contents of the *Historia* were worth reporting, but the data could not be accommodated in the account proper for fear of distorting traditional perceptions.

The bulk of the Insular data interpolated into Sigebert's chronicle derives from Henry of Huntingdon. Robert knew the full text of Geoffrey's *Historia*; indeed in 1139, while a monk at Bec, he had revealed the existence of this startling account to Henry and must have witnessed the burst of enthusiasm recorded in the letter to Warin. There can be no doubt that Robert of Torigni held Henry in very high esteem. At Bec, Robert had a copy of the *Historia Anglorum*, perhaps brought by Henry himself, which covered the years down to 1135. Later, when Robert (now abbot of Mont-Saint-Michel) compiled his chronicle, he used the version extended to 1147.[62] Henry may not have incorporated any substantial amount of Galfridian material into Books 1–3, but one feature of the expanded edition was a new Book 8 which contained the epilogue to the first edition and three epistles, including the letter to Warin.[63] Robert explicitly states that he took Henry's epistolary summary of Geoffrey's account directly from the *Historia Anglorum* (RT, 1:111–12). In other words, it was Henry of Huntingdon who led the way providing a simple expedient for avoiding the difficulties posed by the Galfridian data. Both the letter and the preponderance of the Insular material used by Robert derived from the same unimpeachable source, and it is not reasonable to assume that he doubted the accuracy of one, but not the other.

To some extent the usability of the *Historia regum Britanniae* must be regarded as inversely proportional to the strength of the prevailing views with which the materials were to be integrated. On the other hand, the weight of historical tradition and personal authority had little to do with the quantity or quality of the data reported. There was no reason to believe that a standard source defined the limits of what could be known about the past. Eusebius-Jerome had to be supplemented with regional histories, Bede with the *Anglo-Saxon Chronicle*, and so forth. The traditional overviews of antiquity and the earlier Middle Ages were highly composite and filled with gaps. Both the amount and the coherence of the data in the *Historia regum Britanniae* surpassed the established authorities. As is clear from Robert of Torigni, such superiority could create difficulties, but not all writers assessed the *Historia* in the same way. Although the force of tradition was an important limiting factor in Geoffrey's reception, other considerations tended to complicate matters for twelfth-century historiographers.

Geoffrey of Monmouth offered a plausible explanation for the wealth of new material which he reported. Initially Geoffrey himself could only marvel at the absence of information on early British rule. Gildas and Bede knew nothing of the kings who had reigned before the birth of Christ and even omitted Arthur. The deeds of these men, however, had survived, transmitted orally from generation to generation. The materials of pre-Saxon history had been handed down through a succession of individuals whose memories were as accurate as written record (HRB, c 1, p 71). Ultimately, the data had found inclusion in an extremely old book in the British tongue which Walter, archdeacon of Oxford, asked Geoffrey to translate into Latin (HRB, c 2, p 71).

The ancient book may be a convenient fiction,[64] but Geoffrey's explanation of the potential value of oral tradition is perfectly valid. To suit his own purposes, he credits this mode of transmission with the capacity for preserving historical data intact. Geoffrey claims that his account forms part of a chain of narration which extended unbroken back over Walter's book and various inter-mediaries to actual events. Other twelfth-century writers were more critical in assessing the accuracy of such lore, but no one doubted that certain oral traditions had historical underpinnings.

If Geoffrey's premise is accepted, then the superiority of his data over Continental survivals can be easily rationalized. The traditional, non-Insular view may rest upon unshakeable authority, but, except for Caesar, the writers in question neither witnessed the actual events nor drew on local sources. The historiographic consequences of such remove were familiar to the Middle Ages. Many a work underwent revision and interpolation for precisely this reason.

Jerome added material on Roman history to Eusebius' chronicle, in part because more information was available regionally.[65] Robert of Torigni possessed data on Insular and Norman affairs which had been unknown to Sigebert of Gembloux. The number of examples can be multiplied at will. Indeed, it would be difficult to find a medieval chronicle which did not in some way reflect the advantages of local records and local traditions.

The examples cited make clear that physical location influences a writer's perceptions of history, as well as the availability of data. Jerome's view is Romano-centric, Eusebius' was not. Similarly, Robert concentrates on Anglo-Norman affairs to an extent which Sigebert probably would have found unjustified. Sigebert of Gembloux, however, did regard Insular history as an important component in a much larger framework. He imputed an intrinsic value to Britain's past which earlier Continental writers and particularly the Romans had not done. Nevertheless, the traditional view of the pre-Saxon era depended largely on the conquerors' records, and even a medieval author might reasonably be expected to conclude that the Britons must have viewed their own history through very different eyes. The prevailing notions of British history obviously needed a corrective, one which only local sources could supply. Geoffrey of Monmouth offered just such an Insular viewpoint, purportedly drawn from traditions which rested ultimately on firsthand information.

The appeal of the *Historia regum Britanniae* owes a great deal to Geoffrey's consistently Insular perspective, but despite this unity of viewpoint, not all sections of the account would be handled in the same way by subsequent historians. The mode and incidence of usage vary depending on the presence, strength, and nature of prior views. For the pre-Roman period Geoffrey was the only source of information on Insular affairs, but the situation became more complex in later sections where Geoffrey's perspective was adopted, modified, and even rejected. The factors governing such decisions change with the character of the competing traditions.

Despite the comparative wealth of Continental data on Roman Britain, Geoffrey's version of events enjoyed considerable success. His account was taken as an important corrective to the essentially hostile view of the conquering Romans. The *Historia* offered new insight into the Britons' conduct, but did not deviate from the traditional outline of the epoch's notable occurrences. The two perspectives seemed to complement each other. As a result, Continental authorities and their derivatives, notably Bede, could be used to buttress Geoffrey's account. Corroboration was supplied for the major events and inevitably lent verisimilitude to the Galfridian details. Alfred of Beverley offers an instructive example of such complementary usage.[66] The distribution of Continental materials, however, limited the applicability of this approach to the period of Roman domination.

Beginning with events of the mid-fifth century, local data became available, data which bore directly on the passage of dominion to the Anglo-Saxons. From the appeal to Aetius onwards, Geoffrey no longer represented a counterpoise to a foreign viewpoint but rather an alternative to a parallel Insular tradition. Two competing peoples would be expected to view the same events from different perspectives, but clearly the situation was changing. For the first hundred years of the Anglo-Saxon presence Geoffrey continued to be extraordinarily successful in what he had undertaken. It must be remembered that the only specific event reported by Bede between the Germanic landings and Augustine's mission was the Battle of Mount Badon. The fact that Bede attested to a British resurgence at the close of the fifth century could hardly be considered a problem. The *Anglo-Saxon Chronicle* did convey the impression of a steadily rising curve of Germanic influence, but for writers who drew on Geoffrey, the sparse information contained in these annals could not compete with what the *Historia* recounted about the hero of Mount Badon, the legendary Arthur.

In the *Historia regum Britanniae* the century following the appeal to Aetius is dominated by the rise of the house of Constantine and the reign of Arthur. After the Roman consul has dashed any hope of further military assistance against the Irish and the Picts (HRB, c 91, pp 167–8), the Britons are said to have dispatched Archbishop Guithelinus to Brittany. There he reminds King Aldroenus that the earlier colonization of Armorica with British soldiers is one of the roots of their current dilemma. They are all Britons, and Guithelinus implores the sovereign to accept the British crown and undertake the protection of the island which Rome has abandoned to the barbarians. Aldroenus himself declines, but agrees to send his brother Constantine who does in fact restore the British monarchy (HRB, c 92, pp 168–9).

Constantine's marriage to an unnamed noblewoman is blessed with three sons: Constans, Aurelius Ambrosius, and Utherpendragon – in the order of their birth (HRB, c 93, p 170). When King Constantine is assassinated by a Pict, a dispute develops over the succession. Constans the first-born has entered a monastery, and some favour Aurelius Ambrosius, others Utherpendragon, even though both of the eligible brothers are still only children. While the arguments rage, Vortigern, the *consul Gewisseorum* (HRB, c 94, p 170), persuades Constans to leave the religious life and accept elevation to the throne. When no prelate can be found to anoint Constans, Vortigern, functioning *vice episcopi* (HRB, c 94, p 171), crowns the former monk in a highly irregular ceremony. Not satisfied with simply manipulating the puppet king, Vortigern eventually has Constans killed and assumes the throne himself. Aurelius Ambrosius and Utherpendragon, however, escape to Brittany (HRB, cc 95–6, pp 171–4). Fearing both a campaign on behalf of the rightful heirs and renewed attacks by the Picts, Vortigern turns to the Saxons for help. He does not actually invite Hengist and Horsa, but rather attempts to use the fortuitous arrival of a band of warriors to his own advantage (HRB, cc 97–8, pp 174–6). The hapless Vortigern, however, proves no match for the wily Hengist.[67]

Geoffrey sets the first Germanic landings against a rather different background than did his predecessors. The threat of incursions from the north is still there, but the emphasis has shifted dramatically. Vortigern sits uneasily on the British throne primarily because he is a usurper. His fears over the possible return of the brothers are a much more important factor in determining his actions than are the Picts. Vortigern later finds himself completely unable to restrain the Saxons, and in desperation he attempts to build an impregnable tower. It is in conjunction with this construction that Merlin enters the *Historia*.[68]

The presence of Aurelius Ambrosius and Utherpendragon in Brittany has already created a tendency to look beyond Vortigern, and the prophecies of Merlin reinforce this feature of the account (HRB, cc 109–18, pp 189–203). Following the usurper's death, Aurelius Ambrosius and then Utherpendragon drive back the Britons' foes. Both kings succumb to Saxon treachery, but by this time the *Historia* is moving inexorably toward the reign of Arthur. The dynamics of the Galfridian narrative are such that interrupting the account for a discussion of the early English settlements becomes a virtual impossibility. Writers who drew on Geoffrey simply could not regard the Britons as a negligible force after the arrival of Hengist and Horsa, because to do so would be to discount the deeds of King Arthur.

Geoffrey's portrayal of King Arthur seems to have enhanced what was already a considerable popular reputation. The legendary sovereign gained a new respectability by virtue of his inclusion in the *Historia*, a fact which poets and historians alike would exploit for centuries to come. Despite the existence of contradictory Anglo-Saxon traditions, the *Historia* would prove a potent force in shaping conceptions of British potential and British achievement during the period from the mid-fifth to the mid-sixth century. Geoffrey of Monmouth places Arthur's demise in 542 (HRB, c 178, p 278), some ninety-three years after the date normally assigned to the arrival of Hengist and Horsa.[69] Writers found room for the fabled monarch in an age previously thought to have witnessed only the emergence of the Anglo-Saxon kingdoms. The chronological difficulties posed by conflicting English tradition should not be underestimated, but Arthur's appeal prompted attempts at historiographic compromise of a kind which these selfsame writers were unwilling to make for the post-Arthurian segments.

Beyond the reign of Arthur the attractiveness of the account was not a significant factor. The tenor of British rule deteriorated and the island's future clearly belonged to the Anglo-Saxons. This loss of appeal was not the only significant change with which Geoffrey had to cope. From the sixth century onwards the materials of Insular history improved steadily. Although gaps persisted and uncertainties continued to abound, local record did possess clarity of outline. The *Historia regum Britanniae* entered a period for which the Insular data were better and conventions stronger. Despite the many breaks and frequent confusion, Geoffrey of Monmouth no longer enjoyed the latitude he once did.

At that point where Geoffrey began to concern himself with fixing the chronological limits of British rule, he also had to contend with circumstances far different from those which obtained for earlier sections. Determining the juncture at which dominion passed to the Anglo-Saxons would become a crux, because Geoffrey attempted to exploit what he took to be the vulnerability of contemporary notions regarding the contours of sixth- and even seventh-century Insular history. Geoffrey of Monmouth drew his readers well past the arrival of Hengist and Horsa, and then continued to insinuate a radical British view into the many gaps left by his predecessors, while at the same time paving the way for eventual Anglo-Saxon ascendancy. The undertaking was fraught with difficulties, not all of which he successfully avoided. Geoffrey forced hard choices on twelfth-century writers, and where the post-Arthurian era was concerned, the age and familiarity of Anglo-Saxon tradition came to the fore.

2· A διδαςτις
conscruct

In pre-Galfridian histories there is a close correlation between the establishment of Anglo-Saxon kingdoms and the advent of a new era. The passage of dominion might defy precise dating, but the means by which the invaders had gained ascendancy were clear. Through the founding and gradual expansion of discrete enclaves, Continental Germanic peoples had wrested control of the island from the Britons.[1] Seen in this light the arrival of Hengist and Horsa became extremely important. The entire process could be said to have begun with these two figures. The first landing had led to establishment of the kingdom of Kent, and the pattern was later repeated by other groups. Where these early settlements were concerned, chroniclers had no clear conception of size and socio-political organization. Even to term the first enclaves 'kingdoms' implies a degree of stability and governmental sophistication which the bands of Germanic invaders probably did not achieve for some time. Nonetheless, the basic inference drawn by medieval historians was correct. The several foundings did provide a loose framework for the piecemeal conquest of Britain.

The importance attached to the Anglo-Saxon kingdoms bespeaks a sense that pre-eminence is largely, if not exclusively, a function of territorial control. The available data, however, did not permit any very precise assessment of actual physical domain. This was true of the Germanic enclaves as it was of the lands still under Celtic control. Writers knew that the Anglo-Saxons' gains had been made at the expense of the indigenous Britons, but the borders could not be fixed. Without some determination of the territories held, the relative strength of the contending peoples remained unclear.

When Bede describes the Germanic invasions, more attention is devoted to locating the Continental homelands of the various tribal groups than to specifying the areas which they settled in Britain (HE, 1.15, p 50). So far as the fifth- and sixth-century English kingdoms are concerned, he mentions only a single boundary, the River Humber. This line separates the northern Anglo-Saxon realms from the southern and assumes considerable importance in the *Historia ecclesiastica* because of Bede's concern with the emergence of Northumbria. The fact that the territory controlled by Æthelberht, king of Kent, extended all the way to the Humber is cited as proof of his power (HE, 1.25, p 72; 2.3, p 142). Bede later provides a list of the rulers who held sway over English lands to the south of this river boundary down to the reign of Oswiu (HE, 2.5, pp 148–50). No other borders are discussed for the fifth and sixth centuries, a feature of the account which effectively precludes an assessment of the Britons' position. It is impossible to chart Anglo-Saxon advances in the west and southwest using the testimony of Bede; indeed, he supplies very little information of any kind on the early settlements.

The standard authority for the several histories of the kingdoms was, of course, the *Anglo-Saxon Chronicle*. But despite the annalists' manifest interest in the landings and subsequent foundings, no clear impression of the political map of Britain in the fifth and sixth centuries emerges from the data provided. The recorded contacts with the Britons tend to be military, and an entry which notes that a group of Saxons fought *wiþ Brettas* or *wiþ Walas* at a given location is an uncertain guide to territorial limits.[2] Later writers would equate dominion with control of the heartlands, but they were unable to gauge the progress of the Anglo-Saxons in these terms.

The relative importance of individual occurrences for territorial acquisition and eventual dominion simply could not be determined. In the absence of essential detail the general process tended to take precedence over specific events, but there was no reduction in the data supplied on the enclaves as a result. Had these early settlements been only a springboard for conquest, a passing phenomenon which quickly gave way to unified rule, then some paring down of the available information might have taken place. Subsequent events, however, actually served to underscore the importance of the early enclaves for an understanding of English history. The continuing political fragmentation of the Anglo-Saxons fostered preservation of what was by medieval standards a highly differentiated view of the Germanic conquerors. From Bede onwards, pre-Galfridian writers perceived a need to maintain and even to elaborate distinctions inherent in the surviving data.

This trend stands in marked contrast to the progressive loss of such detail for the Britons. Both Caesar and Gildas supplied at least some information on the tribal and geographical divisions of the Insular Celts.[3] These data, however, disappeared as the sources were reworked from a variety of viewpoints.[4] Later writers deemed such specifics irrelevant to their several historiographic purposes. As a result, the Britons gradually took on a monolithic appearance in the standard sources. The compilation of the *Historia Brittonum* in the ninth century did nothing to correct this erroneous impression, even though the existence of numerous political divisions might have been inferred from certain details.[5] An undifferentiated image of the Britons became firmly established and served to underscore the fragmentation of Anglo-Saxon rule. Where both peoples were concerned, the nature of the data promoted a sense that the early kingdoms had marked a significant break in the island's mode of governance.

The *Historia regum Britanniae* redressed a serious imbalance in the amount of data available on the pre-Saxon past, but Geoffrey of Monmouth did not disabuse his contemporaries of the notion that the Britons constituted an essentially monolithic force in Insular history. Tribal divisions are nowhere mentioned in the *Historia*. The relationship between British kings and their leading subjects can best be described as quasi-feudal, and strong centralized rule remains the consistent ideal. Although dissension and strife may be only too prevalent, it is as a united people that the Britons achieve greatness or near-greatness.[6] The same cannot be said of the Anglo-Saxons, whose early history witnessed major accomplishments under fragmented rule. The appearance of Geoffrey's *Historia* did not mean the end of quasi-institutional periodization. On the contrary, by correlating attainment with the style of government, Geoffrey actually underscored what was already regarded as the principal distinguishing feature of a new era. The Anglo-Saxon kingdoms retained their traditional importance, but the problem of establishing a chronological dividing line became acute.

Although there is much that remains unclear regarding Geoffrey's specific intent, he did not view his account as merely a repository of data. Few medieval history-writers (as distinct from annalists and some chroniclers) did. The *Historia regum Britanniae* is first and foremost a didactic work offering a block of history in light of which subsequent events were to be interpreted.[7] The problems of royal succession, partition, and civil strife which plague the Britons resemble nothing so much as the difficulties of Geoffrey's own day. Walter F. Schirmer has elaborated the close parallels and sees in Geoffrey's depiction a warning of the dangers of civil war.[8] Schirmer's viewpoint is somewhat narrow, but there can be little doubt that for Geoffrey the crucial importance of unified rule was an inescapable lesson of both British and Anglo-Norman history.[9]

Geoffrey's handling of the passage of dominion is consistent with the didactic thrust of his work. The periodization hinges not on the exigencies of the data but on a lesson of history. Time and again Geoffrey of Monmouth depicts the awful consequences of discord and division. Ultimately, however, dominion must pass to a people whose early history was synonymous with fragmented rule. The outcome could not be altered, but neither could historical pre-eminence be gained by virtue of a mode of governance, the folly of which Geoffrey had decried throughout the account. The passage of dominion must not be construed as a demonstration of the superiority of fragmented rule. Quite apart from any ethnic bias harboured by Geoffrey, Anglo-Saxon ascendancy imperiled his entire didactic construct. The Germanic peoples had to be made to triumph despite the lack of unification, not because of it.

In the *Historia regum Britanniae* the Britons lose control of the island as a direct result of their own persistent folly. Geoffrey depicts the Anglo-Saxons as a hostile military presence which is quick to seize the opportunities presented by dissension in the British ranks. Territory passes into the hands of the invaders, but such inroads do not confer historical pre-eminence. Even after the Anglo-Saxons have gained sway over the heartlands, they lack the capacity for giving direction to the island's future. In order to preserve his didactic point, Geoffrey of Monmouth rules out the traditional identification of military conquest with the passage of dominion. As depicted in the *Historia*, the triumph of the Anglo-Saxons results in something less than the promise normally associated with the advent of a new era. The question of territorial control is separated from other considerations, notably the style of government. Geoffrey offers not only a British perspective on familiar events, but a radically different way of determining the moment at which the passage of dominion took place.

To achieve this end, Geoffrey laid the groundwork carefully. The Anglo-Saxons could not be permitted a steady rise to power. The prevailing view of the fifth and sixth centuries emphasized the role of the early kingdoms in the Germanic take-over. If the foundings provided an institutional framework for the conquest, then it might logically be assumed that fragmented rule possessed advantages over the British form of government. In order to forestall such reasoning, Geoffrey of Monmouth broke the chain of inference which led from landing to enclave to achievement. Coventional notions had evolved in the absence of information on the Britons, and Geoffrey simply inserted what purported to be a detailed account of Celtic activities. The fifth and sixth centuries were found to contain British accomplishments which totally eclipsed Anglo-Saxon efforts to gain a foothold on the island. The level of British attainment was seen to depend upon unified rule and affirmed the superiority of centralized government over the fragmentation with which the early English were synonymous. The decline of the Britons in the ensuing epoch was then depicted as a consequence of internal rather than external pressures.

The changes begin with the handling of Hengist and Horsa. For Geoffrey of Monmouth the first Saxon landings were a fateful moment in Insular history. Henceforth the Germanic invaders would constitute an everpresent threat to continued British domination. In the *Historia regum Britanniae*, however, the immediate consequences cannot be graphed as a steadily rising curve of Anglo-Saxon influence and power. Aurelius Ambrosius wrests control of the island from the usurper Vortigern, restoring British rule to its former estate. He inaugurates a glorious era, which culminates in the reign of Arthur. It is not the Saxons who rise during this period, but the Britons. Geoffrey inserts three illustrious rulers from the house of Constantine into the epoch which was formerly thought to have witnessed the emergence of the Anglo-Saxon kingdoms. The deeds of Aurelius Ambrosius, Utherpendragon, and Arthur seem to belie the importance traditionally assigned to these foundings. As an identifying feature of early English rule, the kingdoms play no role in the *Historia regum Britanniae*. Geoffrey confutes the traditional periodization of Insular history and then extends British dominion well beyond Arthur's demise.

As history, the post-Arthurian segments of the *Historia regum Britanniae* are inherently problematic. Geoffrey may have been guided by didactic considerations, but he purported to relate historical data. The success of his fiction brought efforts to reconcile the *Historia* with other sources. Down to the reign of Arthur, writers could do little but note the absence of corroborating testimony. With the arrival of Hengist and Horsa Insular materials began to improve, but the data were meagre and Arthur's appeal too strong. The situation changed when historiographers took up events beyond the mid-point of the sixth century. The chronology in Bede and the *Anglo-Saxon Chronicle* became much tighter, information more plentiful. Geoffrey was cognizant of the altered circumstances and took Insular authority consistently into account. Following Arthur's abdication, the principal sources of the *Historia* are readily identifiable to an extent unparalleled in earlier sections. Geoffrey continued to work in his accustomed manner, but the gaps in existing record had become smaller and far fewer in number. Operating under such constraints tended to make any divergence highly visible. The stage was set for a confrontation between Geoffrey's didactic construct and surviving Insular data. The question of periodization provided the catalyst. At issue was the fixing of a chronological limit to the Britons' long hegemony.

That the tenor of British rule had deteriorated prior to the final loss of dominion was well attested by Gildas. Unlike many other writers, Geoffrey of Monmouth knew the *De excidio* firsthand. According to Gildas, the British resurgence under Ambrosius Aurelianus and the stunning victory at Mount Badon had ushered in a period of relative calm (DEB, cc 25–6, pp 40–1). After years of unrelenting Saxon pressure, the hand of God had stayed the invaders' advance, affording the Britons an opportunity which might not come again. Gildas' compatriots, however, had failed to exploit the stability which resulted from military equilibrium. The peace had endured, but the passage of time rendered the benefits increasingly questionable. The signs of moral decay were everywhere apparent, especially among those whose conduct should set a high standard for the populace as a whole. Freed for a time from the Germanic threat, five tyrannical British rulers had given themselves over to vice and depravity: Constantine, Aurelius Conanus, Vortiporius, Cuneglasus, and Maelgwn (DEB, cc 28–36, pp 41–8).[10]

Gildas treats these kings as ruling over territorial divisions within the British domain. Few historical data are supplied; indeed, Gildas only specifies the regions controlled by two of the rulers.[11] The *De excidio* does not aim to convey any sense of the political map of Britain in the sixth century. There is certainly no reason to suppose that Gildas has provided a complete catalogue of British kings. The tone of the section is homiletic rather than historiographic, and Gildas' handling of the five tyrants would seem to presuppose considerable notoriety. They have been selected because of their moral turpitude, but the flagrant examples of royal misconduct inveighed against by Gildas have not as yet had palpable political or military consequences. Indeed, these kings have been able to persist in their sinful ways, because the peace has endured, obfuscating the long-term historical ramifications of such degeneracy. Although Gildas is acutely aware of the danger posed by the continuing Saxon presence, for the moment at least the danger to the Britons comes from within, not from without.

Although Gildas probably never knew centralized government of the kind envisaged by Geoffrey, the fragmentation represented by the several British kingdoms is an issue of some importance in the *De excidio*. The victory at Mount Badon brought respite from the wars with foreign invaders, but did not mean the cessation of internal strife: 'sed ne nunc quidem, ut antea, civitates patriae inhabitantur; sed desertae dirutaeque hactenus squalent, cessantibus licet externis bellis, sed non civilibus' (DEB, c 26, p 40). Gildas places the blame for this situation squarely on British kings who are quick to wage war, 'sed civilia et iniusta bella agentes' (DEB, c 27, p 41). Aurelius Conanus is later rebuked specifically for his love of civil war (DEB, c 30, p 43). Gildas regards such strife as a major contributory cause of the Britons' failure to seize the opportunity presented by their own resurgence.

The disruptive influence of civil wars can no more be separated from the form of government than can the importance of British kings for the general moral decline. To judge from the *De excidio*, the framework which the Britons have evolved for ruling their domain placed miscreants in positions of power, and promoted a level of internal strife destructive of real progress. Collingwood has advanced the very plausible view that what Gildas records are the consequences of a fundamental change in the government of the island.[12] During the fifth century the Roman system of administration, based on a federation of *civitates*, each with an elected magistrate, gradually gave way to rule by Celtic chieftains. These men, Gildas' *tyranni*, probably came from a less Romanized segment of the populace and brought with them older, barbarian notions of kingship. The proliferation of such realms could be expected to produce both the higher incidence of civil war and the flagrant abuses of power described in the *De excidio*. That the pro-Roman Gildas should view contemporary trends against the background of this development is perfectly reasonable.

Prior to the *Historia regum Britanniae*, the names of Gildas' tyrants do not figure either in Insular or Continental historiography. Bede omitted these rulers, and most later writers, either directly or indirectly, derived their Gildasian materials from the *Historia ecclesiastica*. The compiler of the *Historia Brittonum* knew the *De excidio*, but did not draw on this source for the entries bearing on sixth-century British rule. Gildas had provided little more than the names of the five kings, and the homiletic style of the relevant section hardly lent itself to the kind of historiographic depiction found at this point in the *Historia Brittonum*.[13] The anonymous compiler does mention Maelgwn, but the specific information is not found in the *De excidio* and probably derives from Brittonic sources no longer extant (HB, c 62, pp 205–6).

The use made of Gildas in the *Historia Brittonum* is very revealing. Even if the *De excidio* had circulated more widely, this would not have fundamentally altered the borrowing pattern found in Bede. It is also clear from the *Historia Brittonum* how little information on sixth-century British rule actually gained currency. The few data available could only be given coherent order by employing an Anglo-Saxon regnal list as the underlying framework.[14] Given the paucity of material and the absence of a general outline, Geoffrey's approach to the post-Arthurian era is understandable. Using the Gildasian list of kings, he depicts a period of moral decay for sixth-century British rule. The chronology of the *De excidio* is exceedingly vague, but Geoffrey fixes the onset of this degeneration with some precision. His positioning of the decline hinges on the identification of the Britons' commander at Mount Badon.

Neither Gildas nor Bede names the British leader responsible for the victory on Mount Badon (DEB, cc 25–6, p 40; HE, 1.16, pp 52–4). But by the ninth century, when the *Historia Brittonum* was compiled, the battle had become associated with Arthur, *dux bellorum*. Mount Badon appears as the last and presumably greatest triumph in a list of twelve victories attributed to the legendary commander (HB, c 56, pp 199–200). The *Historia Brittonum* also reports that under Arthur the Britons never suffered defeat at the hands of the

Saxons. This statement would seem to imply a notable career after Mount Badon, but subsequent pre-Galfridian writers restrict their discussions of Arthur's exploits to the twelve canonical battles.

Tales recounting King Arthur's deeds appear to have enjoyed currency during the twelfth century. Although medieval historians do not doubt the historicity of this celebrated monarch, they are alert to the difficulties inherent in the use of popular lore. The oft-quoted statement by William of Malmesbury probably represents the attitude of conscientious historians (GRA, 1.8, 1:11–2). William regards the tales as patently fabulous and separates such lore from veracious histories. The distinction is a familiar one; yet William also knows that the historiographic depictions of Arthur's reign are incomplete. It may be inferred that the Arthur of fables was far more vivid than the historical personage who emerged from the sparse entries of William's predecessors. Nevertheless, he resisted the obvious temptation to supplement his account with material drawn from such popular tales. William implies only that, if the truth were known, the storied ruler would enjoy a loftier position in history. Whatever the historical underpinnings of Arthurian tradition may be, the passage of time has brought many dubious additions and fanciful accretions. Without some basis for selection, William cannot penetrate to the truth. In all likelihood this attitude is responsible for the reluctance of pre-Galfridian historians to move beyond a few well-attested items. Whereas Arthur's victory at Mount Badon belonged to the canon of history, the fables did not, and consequently William restricted himself to this single triumph.

The gap between the historical and the legendary Arthur narrows perceptibly in the *Historia regum Britanniae*. Geoffrey does not give the date of Arthur's accession (cf HRB, c 143, p 228), but a long and very illustrious career follows the Battle of Mount Badon. The *Annales Cambriae* provide justification for placing this triumph some two decades before the events at Camlann involving Modred,[15] and Geoffrey's account reflects a similar notion of the chronological separation between the two occurrences. Consequently, the victory at Mount Badon is assigned to the early portion of Arthur's reign.

The traditional catalogue of victories forms the basis for Geoffrey's depiction of the campaign which a youthful Arthur waged against the Saxons in order to consolidate his position (HRB, cc 143–7, pp 228–34).[16] The climax is the lifting of the siege of Bath. When the Saxons retire to a nearby hill, the British ruler distinguishes himself by the familiar exploits (HRB, cc 146–7, pp 232–4). This battle effectively marks the end of organized Saxon resistance, and pursuit of the fleeing remnants is turned over to Duke Cador of Cornwall, while Arthur hastens northward to aid his nephew Hoel who has been besieged in the town of Alclud by a combined Hiberno-Pictish force (HRB, c 148, pp 234–5). Despite the importance of Mount Badon to the consolidation effort, the victory no longer forms the high point of King Arthur's career. It certainly is not the final memorable triumph of a declining people.

Pre-Galfridian historians assessed Arthur's importance in the context of British resistance to the Anglo-Saxon conquest. He received notice because under his leadership the Britons rallied, albeit briefly. In marked contrast to this essentially parochial view, Geoffrey measures Arthur's greatness on a global scale.[17] The victory at Mount Badon is the prelude to the sovereign's entry into world affairs. King Arthur conquers a vast domain, and ultimately challenges even the authority of Rome. The consolidation of his power in Britain provides a stable base from which he can pursue these larger ambitions. Aurelius Ambrosius and Utherpendragon do not make their influence felt beyond Britain's shores, because a local matter, the Saxon threat, consumes their energies. A unified homeland is a prerequisite for assumption of a major role in history, and Modred's treachery deprives Arthur of this base. The traitorous co-regent divides the people and even the royal household, forcing his uncle to break off the Roman campaign (HRB, cc 176–7, pp 274–6). The early consolidation, of which Mount Badon is a part, figures prominently in Geoffrey's account, but the emphasis has been shifted from the twelve battles themselves to what becomes possible as a result. The final deterioration of British rule must now follow Arthur's abdication in 542. Before departing for Avalon, the wounded monarch hands over the crown to Constantine, the first-named of Gildas' tyrannical kings (HRB, c 178, p 278; DEB, cc 28–9, pp 41–3).

Omitting only Cuneglasus, Geoffrey depicts the reigns of the infamous rulers noted by Gildas. These sovereigns are taken up in the order of their appearance in the *De excidio*, and Geoffrey also borrows the moral failings characteristic of each (HRB, cc 179–83, pp 279–80. Cf DEB, cc 28–36, pp 41–8). In marked contrast to Gildas, the style and tone of the *Historia* are historiographic rather than homiletic, tending to soften the images somewhat. Geoffrey restricts himself to what are purportedly the historical facts and does not inveigh against the kings as Gildas does.[18]

The principal divergence from the *De excidio* has nothing to do with the individual portraits. Geoffrey fashions a line of all-powerful kings out of personages who are described by Gildas as ruling over portions of the British domain. This manipulation of the *De excidio* extends the period of unified British rule well into the second half of the sixth century. Although the Saxons pose a continuing threat, the Britons maintain effective territorial control over the island. Immediately following Arthur's abdication, the Saxons join with Modred's sons but are defeated by Constantine (HRB, cc 179–80, pp 279–80). The description leaves little doubt that the monarch has regained dominion at least over his homeland. The status of foreign lands formerly under King Arthur's control is less clear. Both Aurelius Conanus and Vortiporius are said to reign over the entire island (HRB, cc 181–2, p 280). Malgo (Maelgwn) enlarges his domain by subjugating Ireland, Iceland, Gotland, the Orkneys, Norway, and Denmark (HRB, c 183, p 280). Earlier in the *Historia* Geoffrey describes how Arthur conquered these same six territories on his first campaign beyond Britain's shores (HRB, cc 153–4, pp 238–9). The order in which the lands are mentioned is identical on both occasions. Although the need for reconquest presupposes an earlier loss of control, clearly the military might of the Britons has not suffered in consequence of their rulers' degeneracy. Geoffrey of Monmouth has taken the period of relative calm described by Gildas and turned it into an era of British supremacy under a line of kings who, though flawed, rule over a united people.

What underlies the changes made by Geoffrey is a desire to replace Gildas' image of a fragmented British domain. The five kings named in the *De excidio* do not rule over a unified island, and consequently are inimical to the didactic purpose of the *Historia*. Alterations in so venerable an authority would seem perilous, but these tyrants were long since forgotten by historians accustomed to drawing on the standard sources. Geoffrey of Monmouth picked his spot well, and not even the sharp-eyed William of Newburgh detected the discrepancy.[19]

In the *Historia regum Britanniae* the moral corruption of British rulers is accompanied neither by a diminution of political power nor by the loss of territories. The Britons prevail long after the symptoms of decay first appear. Nevertheless, the signs are highly significant, and Geoffrey of Monmouth uses Gildas' characterizations to isolate what it is that enables the Britons to maintain sovereignty. Success continues to crown British endeavour not because of the various kings' personalities, but because of the island's unity. Centralized government permits direction of the Britons' manifold talents and particularly their military prowess toward common goals. External challenges are easily met, but the real threat comes from within. Britain's unified rule has been corrupted at the core. The governmental framework alone sustains the level of political attainment, and without any inner vitality the situation cannot long endure.

Throughout the *Historia* a monarch's ability to achieve and maintain unity is the touchstone for evaluating his reign. In Geoffrey's view the assumption of a leading role in history presupposes a stable base, and accomplishments endure only so long as the requisite unity. Time and again the Britons indulge a penchant for civil strife which is destructive of their very real historical potential. Even Arthur falls victim to the myopia of his countrymen, and in the post-Arthurian epoch degeneration makes unified rule far more vulnerable than before. When disorder erupts, the circumstances are right for a total collapse.

The first major reversal for the Britons falls in the reign of a man who is 'amator civilium bellorum, invisus Deo et Britonibus' (HRB, c 184, p 281). The British ruler characterized so harshly is Keredic, the fifth king to succeed Arthur. The name occurs elsewhere, but this particular monarch bears little resemblance to any like-named figure.[20] The reign of Keredic is almost certainly Galfridian invention. Indeed, this sovereign serves primarily as the catalyst in a sequence of events centering on a second king, one taken directly from poetic narrative: the legendary Gormund.[21]

Knowing Keredic to be fickle ('cujus inconstantiam comperientes' HRB, c 184, p 281), the Saxons enlist the aid of Gormund, the African king who has conquered Ireland. This pagan ruler crosses over from his own domain and wages war on the Britons. Keredic is driven from city to city, finally taking refuge in Cirencester. Gormund lays siege and is joined by Isembard, renegade nephew of the Frankish king Louis.[22] Again forced to flee, Keredic crosses the Severn into Wales. Neither his subsequent career nor his death is reported. In the absence of organized British resistance the pagan forces roam the countryside at will. After laying waste virtually the entire island, Gormund hands Loegria over to his Saxon allies, and disappears from the account (HRB, cc 184–6, pp 281–3). Whether he returns to Ireland or embarks upon his storied Continental campaign is unclear.

Gormund's depredations produce a break in the continuity of British rule. Those Britons fortunate enough to survive the destruction flee into Cornwall and Wales: 'Secesserunt itaque Britonum reliquiae in occidentalibus regni partibus, Cornubiam videlicet atque Guallias, unde crebras et ferales irruptiones incessanter hostibus fecerunt' (HRB, c 186, p 282). Effective control of their former domain is lost for a lengthy, if somewhat indistinct period of time: 'Amiserunt deinde Britones regni diadema multis temporibus et insulae monarchiam, nec pristinam dignitatem recuperare nitebantur ...' (HRB, c 187, p 283).

The same events produce a corresponding interruption in the exercise of ecclesiastical authority. Gormund's campaign results in the total collapse of organized Insular Christianity. The pagan hordes raze the churches and monasteries in their path. Theonus and Tadioceus, the archbishops of London and York respectively, flee with the surviving priests and precious relics into Wales. A second, very sizable group of clerics sails to Brittany: 'Plures etiam Armoricanam Britanniam magno navigio petierunt, ita ut tota ecclesia duarum provinciarum, Loegriae videlicet et Northamimbriae, a conventibus suis desolaretur' (HRB, c 186, p 283). Christianity survives and even flourishes in the remote areas still under British control, but not in the much larger heartlands. Geoffrey of Monmouth makes this situation the proximate cause of Augustine's mission (HRB, c 188, pp 283–4).

The aftermath of Keredic's reign produces a clear hiatus. The break occurs right before events which Bede depicted as crucial to the subsequent course of English history. With Augustine's arrival imminent and Loegria under Saxon control a new era would seem to be at hand; yet Geoffrey of Monmouth does not shift the focus of his account even temporarily. In the *Historia regum Britanniae* Gormund's depredations produce a spiritual and political vacuum which the Anglo-Saxons are unable to fill.

To Geoffrey's way of thinking, Gormund's Donation would seem to have thrust the Anglo-Saxons to the forefront prematurely. Augustine converts the pagan English, but his mission does not alter the fact that this people is as yet unready to assume the lead in Insular affairs. In both instances benefits are conferred through outside interference. Had the Anglo-Saxons been strong, Gormund would not have been needed to deal with Keredic. Where the conversion is concerned, Geoffrey adopts the view of the British Church. The Anglo-Saxons simply were unworthy to receive the faith.[23] Historical pre-eminence does not follow from gains brought about by outside agency. Identifiably English values neither shape future developments nor give the island a distinctive appearance. Certainly, no characteristic form of government evolves to provide a contrast with British rule. Indeed, the principal obstacle to Anglo-Saxon dominion becomes clear when Geoffrey turns to the island's governance.

Immediately preceding Augustine's arrival, the *Historia regum Britanniae* provides a description of how the Britons and the Saxons governed their respective domains during this period (HRB, c 187, p 283). The two races eschew unified rule and institute parallel systems of tripartite government.[24] There is no indication that the partition of Saxon territories marked an important turning point in the history of the people. Quite the opposite is true. The institution of parallel divisions suggests a parity between the Britons and the Saxons. The balance struck depends not on territorial control, but on the form of government. Divided kingdoms are counted for nought by Geoffrey of Monmouth. Unified rule is the consistent ideal, and by partitioning their lands, the two races betray an identical lack of historical insight.

As Faral has pointed out, Geoffrey shifts principal sources following the depiction of the aftermath of Gormund's campaign (Faral, 2:314). Beginning with Augustine's mission, he draws heavily on Bede.[25] Events are recounted from the Britons' viewpoint, but the *Historia ecclesiastica* becomes the sole recognizable source. In the concluding segments of his history Geoffrey seems bent upon providing something of a counterbalance to Bede. The image projected represents the wilful manipulation and distortion of information in the

Historia ecclesiastica. Geoffrey of Monmouth trades on the gaps in Bede's account, but openly contradicts his source on the key issue of Anglo-Saxon dominion. The net result is two irreconcilable versions of events.

The open contradictions begin with Geoffrey's depiction of a British resurgence following the slaughter at Chester (HRB, c 189, pp 284–5; HE, 2.2, pp 140–2). Meeting in the city which was the site of the massacre, the *principes Britonum* choose Cadfan to lead them against Æthelfrith (HRB, c 190, p 285).[26] A united British force crosses the Humber in pursuit of a foe who has withdrawn to the north. As soon as the movements of the Britons are reported to Æthelfrith, he marches to meet them, but before a pitched battle can be fought, friends of the two parties intercede. A treaty is concluded partitioning Britain at the Humber. Æthelfrith is given control of the lands north of this line, Cadfan the area to the south: 'Deinde, cum catervas suas in utraque parte statuerent, venerunt amici eorum talique pacto pacem inter eos fecerunt, ut Edelfridus trans Humbrum, Cadvanus vero citra fluvium Britanniam possideret' (HRB, c 190, p 286). No mention is made of Anglo-Saxon kingdoms south of the Humber. Cadfan is succeeded by his son Cadwallon (HRB, c 191, p 287), and the Humber remains the boundary between the two peoples until the outbreak of hostilities with Edwin. Cadwallon is driven for a time from his homeland but ultimately gains control of all Britain (HRB, cc 193–201, pp 289–99). Following this reconquest, the balance of power does not shift appreciably in favour of the Saxons until the reign of Cadwaladr.

The notion that the Britons controlled the area south of the Humber from shortly after the slaughter at Chester down to Edwin's day and even beyond directly contradicts Bede. The events at Chester take place during the reign of Æthelberht, king of Kent. Geoffrey describes Æthelberht as *rex Cantiorum* (HRB, c 189, p 284). The kingdom of Kent, however, lies south of the Humber. Bede explicitly states that Æthelberht's rule extends as far as the Humber (*ad confinium usque Humbrae fluminis maximi*), the line which separates the northern Angles from the southern (HE, 1.25, p 72). Indeed, this monarch reigns over all the Angles south of the Humber (HE, 2.3, p 142). Nor is Æthelberht the first English sovereign to do so, but rather the third. When Edwin annexes the southern territories, he becomes the fifth to rule this area. Oswald and Oswiu are the sixth and seventh respectively (HE, 2.5, pp 148–50). Although Bede leaves many territorial questions vague, he is very explicit on Anglo-Saxon dominion south of the Humber. That Geoffrey's account is at variance on this point could not help but attract notice, as William of Newburgh's comments make clear (HRA, 1:13–14). In the *Historia ecclesiastica* the Britons obviously still control certain unspecified regions during the seventh century, but not to the extent described by Geoffrey.

The *Historia regum Britanniae* strips the Anglo-Saxons of dominion over significant portions of the island. By so doing, Geoffrey denies them a leading role in Britain's history until well into the second half of the seventh century. Territorial control is not always a reliable measure of historical influence, but Geoffrey's depiction rules out any other gauge. The Saxons remain what they have been since the time of Hengist and Horsa, a hostile force quick to take advantage of British folly. As a military threat, their importance can be measured only in terms of the lands they control. The Anglo-Saxons react to changes in the character of British rule but do not initiate trends characteristic of the age. Even north of the Humber they do not constitute an identifiable force, shaping the future course of events. Geoffrey's Saxons are a people without contours, much as the Britons appear in earlier accounts. It seems likely that the traditional roles of the two peoples have been consciously reversed.

Paradoxically, Geoffrey's cardboard characterization of the Anglo-Saxons produces considerable uncertainty regarding the point at which they can be said to have gained ascendancy. The confusion stems from the fact that individual preconditions normally associated with this determination are fulfilled at widely scattered chronological points. A people consistently portrayed as a military threat might be expected to assume pre-eminence by force of arms, but such is not the case. In the post-Arthurian segment of the *Historia* victories and defeats alter only the frontiers. The fortunes of war do not confer that order of dominion from which the advent of a new era can be dated. Both for the Saxons and for the Britons the question of territorial control is treated as distinct from other possible indicators. Late in the narrative Geoffrey depicts three moments, any of which under the proper circumstances might serve for the purpose of periodization.

The first such point does involve a shift in the balance of military power and the resultant loss of British control over Loegria. The events are a consequence of Cadwaladr's troubled reign. The poor health of this British monarch precludes firm rule over his ever quarrelsome subjects. Civil war, famine, and finally pestilence ravage the countryside. So heavy is the loss of life that bands of Britons emigrate to other lands; indeed, Cadwaladr himself seeks refuge with King Alan of Brittany (HRB, c 203, pp 299–300). For eleven years the island is virtually uninhabited. Few of the Saxons and Britons who remain behind are able to survive (HRB, c 204, p 301). When the plague has run its course, the Saxons seize the moment. The survivors send word to their Continental homeland that Britain is there for the taking, and the British remnants are powerless to resist the ensuing landings by hordes of Germanic settlers: 'Quod cum ipsis indicatum fuisset, nefandus populus ille, collecta innumerabili multitudine virorum et mulierum, applicuit in partibus Northanunbriae et desolatas provincias ab Albania usque ad Cornubiam inhabitavit' (HRB, c 204, p 301). The extent of the occupation leaves little doubt as to which race exercises effective control over Britain. Any people ruling the territories from Scotland to Cornwall must be regarded as the dominant force. Geoffrey in fact states: 'Ab illo tempore potestas Britonum in insula cessavit et Angli regnare coeperunt' (HRB, c 204, p 301).

Although Geoffrey's statement would seem unambiguous, Saxon domination of Britain's heartlands does not signal the assumption of a pre-eminent role in history. The conquest is an obvious prelude to the ultimate emergence of this people, but Geoffrey plays down any such implications. The entire depiction in the *Historia* militates against construing the take-over as a major Saxon achievement. The Germanic settlers overrun what is essentially a deserted island. Britain has been rendered defenceless by the plague. At the time of the mass emigrations, the Britons voice the belief that the calamities are divine retribution visited on a sinful populace. Cadwaladr enunciates this view in a moving lament (HRB, c 203, p 300), and the interpretation is later confirmed by an angel (HRB, c 205, pp 301–2). The Saxons triumph not by dint of their superiority, but because God has grown weary of British folly. Cadwaladr apostrophizes the Saxons and underscores this fact: 'Non nos fortitudo vestra expellit, sed summi regis potentia, quam nunquam offendere distulimus' (HRB, c 203, p 300). The events are a judgment on the sins of the Britons, not divine approbation of Anglo-Saxon rule.

Following the conquest, Saxon dominion remains devoid of distinguishing features. Geoffrey focuses attention on the Britons, thereby making them identifiable in a way that the conquerors are not. His handling of the two peoples suggests an alternative to the use of territorial control as the prime consideration in fixing the limits of an epoch. A new era may be thought to have begun, either when the Britons lose their character as the determinant force, or when the Saxons assume clear pre-eminence. These two conditions are interrelated but need not be met simultaneously. Geoffrey depicts both moments in Britain's history while separating them chronologically from the military conquest and from each other.

Some time after the Saxon take-over, the Britons gather strength once again. Cadwaladr resolves to return to his homeland and enlists the aid of King Alan of Brittany. As the invasion fleet is being readied, a *vox angelica* orders Cadwaladr to abandon the plan. God no longer wishes the Britons to rule the island. They must await the moment for return prophesied by Merlin. The reoccupation cannot occur until the relics of British saints, removed and hidden away in time of pagan invasion, are restored to their rightful places. For his part Cadwaladr must undertake a pilgrimage to Pope Sergius in Rome, 'ubi peracta paenitentia inter beatos annumeraretur' (HRB, c 205, p 302).

After King Alan has determined that the angelic utterances agree with written oracles, he counsels compliance. The king of Brittany also advises that Cadwaladr's son Yvor and nephew Yni be sent to Britain to rule over the remnants of their people (HRB, c 206, p 302). Following Cadwaladr's death in 689, Geoffrey sketches a period of sixty-nine years during which Yvor and Yni harass the English (HRB, c 207, pp 302–3). The efforts are to no avail, for the Britons have fallen too low. The nadir is reached when this once proud people loses the name borne since the days of Brutus: 'Barbarie etiam irrepente, jam non vocabantur Britones, sed Guallenses, vocabulum sive a Guallone, duce eorum, sive a Gualaes regina, sive a barbarie trahentes' (HRB, c 207, p 303). Merlin's prophecy notwithstanding, the Britons have ceased to constitute a force identified with the future of the island as a whole. The situation is analogous to the renaming of Albion in the wake of Brutus' arrival (HRB, c 21, p 90). Just as the advent of British dominion may be dated from this first name change, so now the reverse would seem to hold true.

Geoffrey mentions only that henceforth the Britons were called the Welsh. The change in appellation mirrors the political realities of the period, but Geoffrey does not provide a corresponding sign of newly won Anglo-Saxon pre-eminence. The omission is noteworthy, because just such an indicator lay close at hand. The island kingdom had borne three names, each associated with an era in its history. Henry of Huntingdon describes Britain as the most noble of islands, 'cui quondam nomen Albion fuit, postea vero Brittannia, nunc autem Anglia' (HA, 1.2, p 6). Henry does not assign dates to these name changes, but their potential usefulness for the periodization of the island's past is clear. Although Geoffrey attaches considerable importance to the renaming of Albion, he does not now signal a passage of dominion by similar means. The name Loegria is used right through to the end of his account as the designation for the heartlands over which the dominant people rules. Geoffrey implies that default by the Britons does not confer pre-eminence on the English. At this point in their history the Anglo-Saxons are not yet worthy of such distinction.

Geoffrey of Monmouth does specify the decisive moment in the history of the Anglo-Saxons, but this juncture lies at some chronological remove from the Britons' loss of name. In the only positive statement made regarding the Germanic peoples who now rule Loegria, Geoffrey lauds their prudent behaviour. The Anglo-Saxons are wiser than the Britons, as they undertake the task of rebuilding the island kingdom: 'At Saxones, sapientius agentes, pacem et concordiam inter se habentes, agros colentes, civitates et oppida reaedificantes, et abjecto sic dominio Britonum, jam toti Loegriae imperaverant, duce Adelstano, qui primus inter eos diadema portavit' (HRB, c 207, p 303). Geoffrey judges the Saxons against the same standard consistently applied to the Britons. The institution of unified rule under Athelstan fulfils the prerequisite for assumption of a dominant role in Insular affairs.

Geoffrey's comment on Athelstan immediately follows the renaming of the Britons in the text, but the chronological interval between the two occurrences is considerable. Given the arrangement of materials in the *Historia,* it would seem reasonable to connect the name change with the end of the period of guerrilla warfare begun by Yvor and Yni. Geoffrey explicitly states that these tactics were used against the Saxons for sixty-nine years following the death of Cadwaladr in 689. If the inference is correct, then the new appellation would have gained currency in the mid-eighth century. Athelstan's accession falls in the year 924. Over a century and a half appear to separate the two events.[27]

Although the Britons have not exercised territorial dominion since the early years of Cadwaladr's reign, Geoffrey denies the Anglo-Saxons pre-eminence until the tenth century. The statement regarding Athelstan reflects a tradition that the Battle of Brunanburh heralded the passing of a style of government.[28] Prior to this triumph Anglo-Saxon rule was seen as a complex of interrelationships between autonomous and semi-autonomous kingdoms. Under Athelstan the fragmentation which had prevailed since the original Germanic enclaves yielded to strong central government.[29] Throughout the *Historia regum Britanniae* Geoffrey stresses the importance of unified rule. Just as on earlier occasions a divided kingdom prevents the Britons from assuming a leading role in history, so now the Saxons are counted for little until the advent of centralized control. Geoffrey is entirely consistent, but the choice of this turning point is dictated by a lesson of history, not by the exigencies of available data.

Viewed in the context of Insular history as a whole, Athelstan's accession is not a usable point from which to date the advent of Anglo-Saxon dominion. It must be remembered, however, that the *Historia regum Britanniae* provides a systematic record of events only down through the reign of Cadwaladr. In the closing sections of the account Geoffrey need no longer be concerned with gaps in the chronology. He can range at will, isolating moments of particular importance. The criterion used in the selection is didactic and ignores certain familiar features of English history. To deny the Anglo-Saxons pre-eminence until the reign of Athelstan would eliminate two rather clearly delineated epochs: the period of the early kingdoms and the era of the Danish invasions.

By skipping over the eighth and ninth centuries, Geoffrey creates the impression of a historical vacuum, a vast interregnum between periods of unified rule. Events in the interim are accounted of little significance, because the style of government promotes civil strife inimical to major achievement. That Geoffrey's interpretation has a basis in fact cannot be denied. The consequences of political fragmentation are readily apparent in early English history. Internal struggles did tend to consume Anglo-Saxon energies, precluding a significant political role on the Continent and beyond. The Danish invasions brought turmoil of a different kind, but the lack of unity on the part of the English facilitated foreign incursion by impeding combined military operations. Factionalism is a prime determinant throughout much of Anglo-Saxon history.

Geoffrey of Monmouth sought to exploit the absence of an early high point in English history. He attributed this lack to the fragmentation of Anglo-Saxon rule down to the tenth century. His didactic end could only be achieved by separating historical pre-eminence from the entire question of territorial dominion. To equate control of the heartlands with the assumption of a leading role in Insular affairs would only have served to underscore the importance of the nascent kingdoms as providing the governmental framework for the Germanic conquest. This traditional association is precisely what Geffrey controverts. The twelfth century, however, accorded the periodization in the *Historia regum Britanniae* a mixed reception. Geoffrey was moderately successful in extending the period of British rule beyond the arrival of Hengist and Horsa, but no twelfth-century writer accepted the premise upon which his didactic construct rested. It would prove virtually impossible to abandon the notion that dominion passed with territorial control, particularly when attempts were made to reconcile the Galfridian version of events with the testimony of English authorities.

3· compilation
and compromise

In the years following the appearance of the *Historia regum Britanniae* the passage of dominion from the Britons to the Anglo-Saxons became a matter of active concern, especially to compilers of historical surveys. For writers who sought to incorporate Geoffrey's account into a systematic overview of Insular history, the task of fixing the duration of British rule entailed momentous decisions regarding the reliability of available sources. At issue were the familiar contours of a crucial segment of Britain's past. The Galfridian periodization challenged conventional thinking not only on the Britons, but also on the Anglo-Saxons. Geoffrey stripped the English of significant achievement during the period which extended from the first Germanic invasions all the way to Athelstan's accession. Some traditions proved more vulnerable than others, and, as a result, the impact of the *Historia* was not felt uniformly along the entire length of the time-span treated in the account. Twelfth-century writers were, however, prepared to adjust the dividing line between eras. Those compilers who made Geoffrey the basis for a depiction of pre-Saxon history located the passage of dominion well after the arrival of Hengist and Horsa but did not forsake prior authority entirely. Pre-Galfridian views on the gradual emergence of the Anglo-Saxons were sufficiently vague to provide ample room for compromise. Final placement of the demarcation depended upon individual assessments of the weight to be assigned to various sources and traditions.

The problems faced by historians who sought accommodation between the Galfridian and Anglo-Saxon perspectives can best be understood by an examination of Henry of Huntingdon's *Historia Anglorum*. This influential work was the most systematic survey of its day and the first to give serious consideration to the pre-Saxon era. Henry offered a composite picture, one which integrated the testimony of standard authorities into a coherent overview. No pre-Galfridian writer paid greater attention to matters of structure, and consequently the *Historia Anglorum* affords considerable insight into the factors which shaped subsequent trends in the handling of the passage of dominion.

Down through the end of Book 3 Henry's account bears witness to the great weight of Bede's authority, where contemporary notions regarding the rhythms of early Insular history are concerned.[1] This portion of the *Historia Anglorum* covers the same time-span treated systematically in the *Historia regum Britanniae*. Reader awareness of Bede's underlying importance to the structure of the *Historia Anglorum* is inversely proportional to the availability of supplemental data. So long as Continental sources provide a comparative abundance of information, the historical foreground tends to obscure the frame being used by Henry. But with the departure of the Roman legions comes a loss of these supplementary materials and obtrusive dependence on Bede.

Recounting the events which led up to the first Anglo-Saxon landing, Henry of Huntingdon follows the contours and even wording of the *Historia ecclesiastica* closely. Unable to defend themselves against the Irish and the Picts, the Britons appeal to the Roman consul Aetius (HA, 1.46, p 35; HE, 1.13, p 46). When the last hope of mortal assistance is dashed, the Britons place their trust in God. They embark upon a campaign of guerrilla warfare, and finally prevail (HA, 1.46, pp 35–6; HE, 1.14, pp 46–8). Peace and prosperity, however, bring moral decline and little respite. The next spate of Hiberno-Pictish incursions finds the Britons an enfeebled people. Vortigern turns to the Saxons for help, and the call for assistance brings Book 1 to a close (HA, 1.47, pp 36–7; HE, 1.14, p 48).

For Henry of Huntingdon the arrival of Hengist and Horsa inaugurates a new era in Insular history. His account of the Germanic invasions rests heavily on Bede (HA, 2.1, pp 38–9; HE, 1.15, pp 48–50), but the primary function of Book 2 is to accommodate data not found in the *Historia ecclesiastica*. The supplemental materials in question derive ultimately from the *Anglo-Saxon Chronicle*. Book 2 of the *Historia Anglorum* traces the foundings and early histories of the kingdoms of the Heptarchy, a phenomenon which Henry regarded as the prime identifying feature of English rule.

In the prefatory section of Book 1 the importance of these kingdoms has already been signalled. Henry of Huntingdon begins the relevant chapter with his famous comments on the foreign invasions which punctuate Britain's history: 'Quinque autem plagas ab exordio usque ad præsens immisit ultio divina Brittanniæ, quæ non solum visitat fideles, sed etiam dijudicat infideles ...' (HA, 1.4, p 8). The five plagues provide a series of natural divisions and are a key element in the structure of the *Historia Anglorum*.[2] After enumerating the foreign incursions, Henry states: 'Quando autem Saxones hanc terram sibi subjugaverunt, reges septem statuerunt, regnisque nomina pro libitu imposuerunt' (HA, 1.4, p 8). The wording is very revealing, because England's toponymy obviously has reinforced the significance of these kingdoms for an understanding of Insular history. Henry then lists the kingdoms together with their principal cities, but no attempt is made to fix the historical position of the Heptarchy with any chronological precision. The prefatory section of Book 1 catalogues the characteristic features of Britain's geography and history. The function of this segment of the *Historia Anglorum* is descriptive, and Henry limits the information accordingly. The early histories of the kingdoms are taken up in Book 2, but from the outset Henry leaves little doubt that the Heptarchy constitutes an important marker.

On the authority of the *Anglo-Saxon Chronicle* the emergence of this characteristic means of government is placed in the century and a half following the initial landings. Bede posed no obstacle to the insertion of such a large block of material, because he had assigned only one event, namely the Battle of Mount Badon, to the period between the Germanic invasions and Augustine's mission. The chronology in this section of the *Historia ecclesiastica* is enormously compressed, and in Book 2 of the *Historia Anglorum* Henry merely expands the depiction, using the data from the *Anglo-Saxon Chronicle*.

The inclusion of the material on the Heptarchy does not herald the end of Bede's structural importance. On the contrary, Henry interrupts the consideration of secular developments to devote Book 3 to the institution of the apostolic faith. Although the *Anglo-Saxon Chronicle* duly notes Augustine's mission (ASC, p 14), there is no indication that this event possessed epochal significance, or that the conversion of the English merited separate treatment. The annalists simply inserted items bearing on religious history at the appropriate point in the chronology. The *Historia Anglorum* represents an attempt at compromise between two views of Insular developments. Whereas Book 2 bears witness to the importance of the *Anglo-Saxon Chronicle* for assessing the early kingdoms, Book 3 attests to the continuing impact of Bede's personal authority.

Although Henry regarded the two sources as compatible, correlating the accounts posed something of a problem. The year 597 did not mark a convenient point to interrupt the discussion of early English rule. Bede and the Anglo-Saxon annalists tended to complement each other because of the exclusivity of their respective viewpoints, but it must be remembered that down to this point the early histories of the kingdoms were inserted into a gap. The seventh century offered the first significant overlap between Henry's principal sources. Rather than attempt to incorporate the history of the conversion into the framework of the *Anglo-Saxon Chronicle*, Henry of Huntingdon treated this subject separately. He seems caught between the perceived importance of the Heptarchy and the epochal significance assigned to Augustine by Bede. The solution to the difficulty is interesting in light of the periodization subsequently proposed by Geoffrey of Monmouth.

In Book 2 of the *Historia Anglorum* the emergence of the Anglo-Saxon kingdoms is traced down to the time of Caedwalla. His accession and conquest of the Isle of Wight are the last events reported in Book 2 (HA, 2.39, p 63). Henry now jumps back in time over a century to provide the background for Augustine's mission. Book 3 picks up Bede's account of the conversion with events of the year 582 (HA, 3.1, p 67; HE, 1.23, p 68).[3] The progress of the faith is then followed into the reign of Caedwalla. The Isle of Wight is the final territory to receive Christianity, and Henry also brings Book 3 to a close with the conquest and conversion of this island (HA, 3.50, p 103). Subsequent events of Caedwalla's brief reign, including his death in Rome, are treated in Book 4 (HA, 4.3, p 105; 4.5, pp 106–8).

Henry's information on Caedwalla derives from Bede's *Historia ecclesiastica* and from the *Anglo-Saxon Chronicle*. Both sources report the conquest of the Isle of Wight, but only Bede notes: 'Hoc ergo ordine, postquam omnes Brittaniarum prouinciae fidem Christi susceperant, suscepit et insula Uecta ... ' (HE, 4.16, p 382). The *Anglo-Saxon Chronicle* omits any reference to the conversion of the Isle of Wight and attaches no particular importance to the conquest of this island for the early history of English rule (ASC, p 24). Henry's use of Caedwalla's campaign as a dividing line is without close parallel in either source. The arrangement of materials in the *Historia Anglorum* would seem to reflect the continuing effort to correlate two rather different views of crucial developments in the seventh century. In all likelihood Henry of Huntingdon began with Bede's comments on the conquest of the Isle of Wight and then used the significance of this event for the spread of the apostolic faith to impose a division on the running account in the *Anglo-Saxon Chronicle*.

The Caedwalla in question is, of course, Geoffrey's Cadwaladr, the king whose reign brings the systematic portion of the *Historia regum Britanniae* to a close. Geoffrey of Monmouth explicitly identifies this figure as the ruler 'quem Beda Chedwaldam juvenem vocat' (HRB, c 202, p 299). The passing of Caedwalla/Cadwaladr falls in 689 (HE, 5.7, p 470; HRB, c 206, p 302), two hundred and forty years after the arrival of Hengist and Horsa, the event with which Henry of Huntingdon began his treatment of Anglo-Saxon history.[4] Geoffrey and Henry may both draw on Bede, but their views on periodization are obviously incompatible.

In the letter to Warin, Henry reacts with enthusiasm to the *Historia regum Britanniae*. The missive is a simple epitome, and the tone suggests composition rather soon after the startling discovery at Bec. Henry indicates neither distrust of Geoffrey's veracity nor areas of disagreement with the *Historia Anglorum*.

Geoffrey's regnal list serves as the frame for the epistle, and Henry follows the outline through to the death of Cadwaladr.[5] At this point he observes: 'Exinde Britanni et nomen et regnum penitus amiserunt' (RT, 1:111). Robert of Torigni would later add: 'Ex tunc illa Britannia est Anglia nominata' (RT, 1:111). Cadwaladr's demise is taken as effectively marking the passage of dominion. Henry of Huntingdon knows full well the identity of this ruler and provides Warin with the essential information: 'Tandem Chedwalladrus regnavit, quem Beda Chedwallam vocat, filius Chedwallonis et sororis Pendæ' (RT, 1:111). The epistle makes no mention of Athelstan.

That Henry of Huntingdon should offer no comment on a depiction which diverged so radically from his own is remarkable. The *Historia Anglorum* and the *Historia regum Britanniae* agreed in general outline only down to the first Saxon landings. Henry composed the letter in response to Warin's query regarding British rule prior to Caesar's expeditions (RT, 1:97). For all subsequent events Warin could have been referred to the *Historia Anglorum*, a work apparently known to him. That Henry found it necessary to summarize the contents of Geoffrey's entire account must be attributed to the enormous impact of the *Historia regum Britanniae*. The tone of the missive does not bespeak sober reflection on the implications of Geoffrey's depiction. Rather, the letter seems to provide an outlet for Henry's genuine fascination with an account only recently discovered.

Henry's initial reaction to the *Historia regum Britanniae* stands in marked contrast to his subsequent use of this new source. Although Henry of Huntingdon revised the *Historia Anglorum* repeatedly, no fundamental changes were made in Books 1–3. The post-1139 recensions do bear the impress of Geoffrey's history, but Henry contented himself with very minor additions.[6] Even Arthur's appeal failed to overcome the apparent reserve. Book 2 of the *Historia Anglorum* already contained a brief report on Arthur's career, but only the twelve famous victories were described (HA, 2.18, pp 48–9). Given the appeal of the materials, substantial revision might have been expected. At issue, however, was far more than the simple interpolation of additional data. In the *Historia Anglorum* Book 2 chronicled the emergence of the Heptarchy. Henry depicted a steadily rising curve of Anglo-Saxon influence, beginning with the arrival of Hengist and Horsa. Arthur's twelve triumphs were but a brief interruption in this development, not the first high point in a glorious period of British rule. Geoffrey may or may not have had Henry's work specifically in mind as a target, but certainly the view of Insular history presented in the *Historia Anglorum* is the same one countered in the *Historia regum Britanniae*. Just as Geoffrey's didactic construct precluded detailed consideration of the Anglo-Saxon kingdoms, so too Henry's composite depiction had no place for the achievements of the house of Constantine. The two accounts were mutually exclusive.

Henry of Huntingdon does not discuss the myriad problems which accommodation with Geoffrey would have posed. The decision to exclude all but the most inconsequential items bespeaks an awareness of the difficulties. It cannot be said, however, that the letter to Warin represents a level of interest which dropped appreciably after Henry had time to reflect upon the implications of the Galfridian construct. The epistolary summary of Geoffrey's *Historia* found inclusion in the new Book 8 of the expanded edition of the *Historia Anglorum*, together with two other letters: 1/ a discussion of the lines of succession in the world's ancient kingdoms (addressed to Henry I); and 2/ the well-known *De contemptu mundi*. Henry obviously regarded these epistles as valuable addenda, valuable enough to justify interrupting the chronological flow of his own account. Partner has underscored the centrality of *De contemptu mundi* for Henry's entire view of history,[7] but the letter on world rulers is more germane to the matter at hand. Henry of Huntingdon does not differentiate between the standard information addressed to Henry I and the Galfridian version of British history. Neither body of material could be incorporated into the running account of the *Historia Anglorum*, but that fact apparently did not detract from the interest and importance of the data. If Henry harboured doubts as to Geoffrey's veracity, no trace of such misgivings has survived.

Although the *Historia Anglorum* does not offer an example of attempted integration, it does illustrate the basic conflict between the English and Galfridian views of the fifth, sixth, and seventh centuries. From the initial Saxon landings onwards, Bede and the *Anglo-Saxon Chronicle* provided the foundation for a very different interpretation of Insular developments. To varying degrees and often with surprising results, the constituent elements in Henry's depiction continued to shape and curtail the use of the *Historia regum Britanniae*.

Around the time of Henry's visit to Bec, Geffrei Gaimar seems to have drawn extensively on the *Historia regum Britanniae* for the pre-Saxon segment of his ambitious vernacular history. Gaimar's depiction originally surveyed events from Jason's quest for the Golden Fleece down to the death of William Rufus.[8] The early portions of the text have not survived, including the section on the era of British dominion. Inevitably a great deal remains uncertain regarding the precise extent of Gaimar's dependence on Geoffrey's *Historia*, but it is possible to infer from the *Estoire des Engleis* how the periodization was handled.

In the epilogue Gaimar describes the compilation of his history, a project which he undertook at the behest of the Lady Constance (EDE, lines 6430–1, p 203). She was the wife of Ralph Fitz Gilbert, the well-connected member of an old Lincolnshire family.[9] When Gaimar encountered difficulties obtaining the *Historia regum Britanniae*, Ralph borrowed a copy from Walter Espec, lord of Helmsley. The text had come into Walter's hands from Robert earl of Gloucester, one of the individuals to whom Geoffrey of Monmouth dedicated the *Historia* (EdE, lines 6439–52, p 204). On the basis of information supplied in the epilogue, Alexander Bell dates the composition of Gaimar's work 'towards the close of the five-year period 1135–40' (EdE, pp li-lii). Although the exact completion date of Geoffrey's *Historia* cannot be ascertained, the range most frequently discussed is relatively small – 1136 to 1139. Gaimar may well have begun his own compilation without the Galfridian depiction of Britain's past. When he did obtain a copy, the *Historia* apparently had not yet gained wide circulation beyond the immediate circle of individuals to whom Geoffrey had dedicated the account. Gaimar states that he collated *le livere Walter Espac* (Geoffrey's *Historia*) with a second book already in his possession: 'Le bon livere de Oxeford/Ki fust Walter l'arcediaen' (EdE, lines 6458–9, p 204). Depending on the timing, Geffrei Gaimar may or may not have relied heavily on Geoffrey of Monmouth throughout the depiction of British history. If current estimates of the speed of composition are accurate, then any delay in acquiring the text could have had a considerable impact.[10]

Be that as it may, Gaimar does seem to have followed Geoffrey closely for the Battle of Camlann. Moreover, King Arthur's conquest of Denmark figures prominently in the Haveloc story, a fact which bespeaks reliance on the *Historia* for the early portion of Arthur's reign as well.[11] How far such dependence extended back into pre-Arthurian British history is most unclear. What militates against postulating too great a similarity is the partial transmission of Gaimar's work. The *Estoire des Engleis* survives in four manuscripts, and in each case the text is preceded by Wace's *Roman de Brut*. This arrangement would seem to suggest that Gaimar's early effort was supplanted by the more Galfridian Wace.[12]

Gaimar treats English and Anglo-Norman history as distinct from what has gone before. The first thirty-eight lines of the *Estoire des Engleis* form a prologue seemingly analogous in function to the *prologi* with which medieval authors frequently begin individual books in longer histories. This is not to say that Gaimar's work was originally divided into books, but only that he clearly marked the end of at least one era in Insular history. No similar line is drawn between the Anglo-Saxon and Norman periods (cf EdE, lines 5241–352, pp 166–70). Although the lost portions of the text may have contained other equally sharp divisions, the *Estoire des Engleis* hardly warrants the assumption that such demarcations were a regular feature of Gaimar's depiction.

The surviving prologue originally served as a transition between two major segments of the account.[13] There can be little doubt that the existence of such a division facilitated the substitution of Wace's *Brut* for Gaimar's own depiction. The first thirty-eight lines of the *Estoire des Engleis* have both a retrospective and an anticipatory function. They look back to the close of the previous epoch and forward to the developments which will shape the coming era. This twofold purpose is again reminiscent of book-prologues in larger medieval histories. Gaimar uses the opening lines to sketch the historical context, and his views on the question of periodization may be inferred with a fair degree of certainty. The implications for the reception of the *Historia regum Britanniae* are extremely interesting.

The opening lines of the prologue refer to events previously depicted, namely the accessions of Constantine and Yvain:

> Oïd avez cumfaitement
> Costentin ot cest casement
> E cum Yvain refait fu reis
> De Mureif e de Loeneis.
> (EDE, lines 1–4, p 1)

In Geoffrey's *Historia* kingship is thrust upon these two individuals in the wake of Modred's rebellion. When Arthur lands at Richborough, the insurgents and their allies inflict heavy casualties. Among the fallen is King Auguselus, whom Yvain succeeds (HRB, c 177, pp 275–6). Later, after the defeat of Modred's forces in the Battle of Camlann, Constantine receives the crown of Britain from a wounded Arthur (HRB, c 178, p 278). Gaimar begins with the aftermath of King Arthur's demise and obviously derives his information from Geoffrey of Monmouth.

There has always been a strong presumption that Gaimar followed Geoffrey's *Historia* only down through the accession of Constantine and that the Battle of Camlann was taken as marking the effective loss of British dominion. Scholars have tended to be cautious in their formulations, holding open the possibility that the prologue may recall not the most recently depicted events, but much earlier matters which only now have become important, as Gaimar prepares to consider the Anglo-Saxons. Later manuscript compilers used the prologue in this fashion. The first thirty-eight lines are retained in three out of four cases, even though the *Roman de Brut* precedes the *Estoire des Engleis*.[14] Wace followed Geoffrey through to the end, and the fact that compilers kept the prologue under these circumstances could conceivably reflect the usage in Gaimar's history. The *Estoire des Engleis* may open with the aftermath of the Battle of Camlann, but that would not in itself preclude Gaimar's having followed the outlines of the *Historia* beyond Arthur's departure for Avalon.

The manuscript evidence is inconclusive; indeed, one aspect of these compilations would seem to render the importance of such witnesses dubious at best. Wace's *Brut* begins with the life and deeds of Brutus, not with Jason and the Golden Fleece. In light of the two very different starting points, I can see no particular reason for thinking that a compiler would only substitute one work for another if they ended at precisely the same juncture. The mechanical arrangement of discrete texts in a codex to form a historical survey is commonplace in the Middle Ages, but a completely coherent overview seldom results. Although an effort may be made to dovetail the several accounts, gaps frequently occur, as do significant areas of overlapping testimony. If Wace's greater dependence on Geoffrey prompted the substitution, then a prime consideration might well have been the fact that the *Roman de Brut* offered a vernacular paraphrase of the entire *Historia*, while Gaimar abandoned the Galfridian version of events well before the end.

In assessing the likelihood that the *Historia regum Britanniae* was followed only down through the accession of Constantine, the substantive differences between Gaimar's depiction of the post-Arthurian era and Geoffrey's have been overlooked. When the *Estoire des Engleis* opens, events may be tied to the Galfridian regnal list through the figure of Constantine, but the image of the mid-sixth century bears little resemblance to the situation described in the *Historia*. The two accounts diverge on the question of unified British rule, a point on which Geoffrey was at variance with all prior authorities.

Geffrei Gaimar explicitly denies a continuance of the strong centralized government which the Britons enjoyed under Arthur. In the wake of Camlann, Britain has become an island divided. Yvain holds sway over Moray and Lothian in Scotland but is effectively cut off from Constantine by the English. To gain an ally against King Arthur, Modred ceded control of the area north of the Humber to the Saxons. As a result of these territorial concessions, the English were able to seize all the land formerly held by Hengist, thereby acquiring a viable base for future expansion (EdE, lines 1–14, p 1). The Celtic peoples of Britain have entered a dark era in their history, a time of desperate troubles and perpetual strife. Reinforced from the Continent, the Saxons would conquer the island piecemeal. The process encompasses an unspecified period of time and ends when Britain is renamed England (EdE, lines 15–32, pp 1–2).

In the *Estoire des Engleis* Constantine's reign marks the start of developments which will eventually bring Anglo-Saxon ascendancy. Gaimar measures political power in territorial terms, and Modred's Donation is depicted as the key to what follows. The actual take-over will be accomplished gradually, but English expansion depends upon circumstances created by the rebellion against Arthur. Gaimar establishes a direct causal link between Modred's treachery and English domination.

The political consequences of Modred's treasonous designs are far more significant in the *Estoire des Engleis* than in the *Historia regum Britanniae*. For Geoffrey of Monmouth the abdication of King Arthur is, to be sure, a fateful event. Moral deterioration begins almost immediately, but the decline is hardly precipitous. The Britons maintain unified rule over their homeland for a considerable period of time. The passage of dominion is finally brought about by persistent British folly. Modred exemplifies a myopia which will one day result in forfeiture of pre-eminence in Insular affairs, but his rebellion is not the proximate cause of Anglo-Saxon ascendancy.

Gaimar borrowed Modred's Donation directly from the *Historia regum Britanniae* (HRB, c 177, p 275), but in Geoffrey's account the entire matter is laid quickly to rest. Immediately following Constantine's accession, Modred's two sons and their Saxon allies attempt to overthrow the new king but are defeated in a series of battles. The unnamed sons of Arthur's infamous nephew flee along separate routes, and Constantine must hunt them down individually. He slays each of the brothers before the altar of God, one in Winchester and one in London. Four years later divine retribution is visited on Constantine for the sacrilege, but not before this monarch has ensured the continuance of unified British rule (HRB, cc 179–80, pp 279–80).

Despite the obvious centrality of the rebellion and subsequent killings to Constantine's rather brief reign, Gaimar makes no mention of these events. Geoffrey of Monmouth borrowed the sacrilege from the *De excidio*. The account in the *Historia* represents a free adaptation of Gildas' statement that Constantine murdered two royal children, while they were in the bosoms of two mothers, the Church and their mother after the flesh (DEB, c 28, pp 41–2). Gaimar eliminates the desecration of the altar of God entirely; indeed, he gives no indication that Constantine is anything but a worthy, if embattled, successor to Arthur. The moral thrust of the characterization, shared by Gildas and Geoffrey of Monmouth, disappears in the *Estoire des Engleis*. The Britons' position has become precarious following Arthur's demise, but not because of Constantine's personal failings. The root of the problem is Modred's Donation. Leaving aside the question of centralized British rule, Gildas and Geoffrey of Monmouth depict the mid-sixth century as a time of relative stability when the Britons held the Saxons in check. This image of the era is gone from the *Estoire des Engleis*, replaced by constant strife and steady Saxon expansion. An unspecified period of time will pass before Britain finally loses her name and is called England, but Gaimar places the start of these fateful developments in Constantine's reign.

As Alexander Bell has pointed out, Constantine functions as a 'chronological peg.'[15] At the opening of the *Estoire des Engleis* this monarch serves to place events relative to the regnal list in the *Historia regum Britanniae* and then disappears from the account. Constantine provides the principal connecting link with the preceding compositional block, in which Gaimar appears to have followed Geoffrey of Monmouth closely at least for King Arthur's reign. Beyond the data found in the prologue, very little information is supplied on Constantine. He belongs to the historical backdrop and does not figure in the events recounted. Gaimar, however, has no intention of skipping over the turmoil of the mid-sixth century. On the contrary, he uses the welter of competing interests to press the claim of a third ethnic group, the Danes.

Although the principal source for the *Estoire des Engleis* is the *Anglo-Saxon Chronicle*, Gaimar begins the account proper with the tale of Haveloc. Before bringing the prologue to a close, he effects a transition to Danish involvement in Insular affairs:

> E les nevoz Arthur regnerent
> Ki encuntre Engleis guerïerent
> Mes li Daneis mult les haeient
> Pur lur parenz ki mort esteient
> Es batailles que Arthur fist
> Cuntre Modred qu'il puis ocist.
> (EDE, lines 33–8, p 2)

Relations between Britain and Denmark during the reign of King Arthur form a backdrop against which the Haveloc story is set. Not only do general attitudes depend upon the recent past, but also the hero's predicament at the start of the tale.[16]

Of interest here, however, is the political fragmentation described by Gaimar as he turns to Haveloc's rise from kitchen boy to king. South of the Humber strong centralized government does not mark Constantine's reign. Two kings, Adelbrit the Dane and Edelsi the Briton, rule over very sizable domains in the British heartlands.[17] Gildas' authority is invoked to warrant the existence of such territorial divisions under Constantine:

> Se ço est veir que Gilde dit
> En la geste trovai escrit
> Que dous reis ot ja en Bretaine,
> Quant Costentins ert chevetaine,
> Cil Constentins li niés Arthur
> Ki ot l'espee Kalibur.
> (EDE, lines 39–44, p 2)

The two sovereigns in question, Adelbrit and Edelsi, belong to the tale of Haveloc and are not to be found in any extant source which antedates the *Estoire des Engleis*. Gaimar's concern centres on the character of Constantine's reign rather than on the identity of these kings. Gildas serves as guarantor only for the depiction of a fragmented British domain.

Given the fact that Gaimar diverges from Geoffrey on the entire question of unified British rule, the Gildas reference is extremely interesting. By means of Constantine, Geffrei Gaimar links the Haveloc story to the chronology in the *Historia regum Britanniae* at a point where the *De excidio* is not only the sole recognizable source, but is actually being manipulated. It will be recalled that Geoffrey of Monmouth extended the period of centralized British control over the entire island by fashioning a line of succession out of kings described by Gildas as ruling over portions of the Celtic domain. I believe that Gaimar recognized the source of Geoffrey's Constantine and invoked Gildas' authority in order to justify the introduction of two seemingly autonomous kingdoms into a period which the *Historia regum Britanniae* describes as a time of unified British rule.[18]

Gaimar's brief sketch of the worsening situation in Constantine's day bears little resemblance to the period of calm depicted by Gildas. The balance of power is entirely different, moral censure completely absent. Gaimar does not cite Gildas in preparation for making the *De excidio* the basis for the handling of subsequent events. The immediate reason for the appeal is the prominence given two non-English kingdoms in the Haveloc story. Little can be inferred with any certainty regarding the form in which Gaimar found this tale, but Bell leaves no doubt on one point: Geffrei Gaimar added the Arthurian backdrop upon which placement of Haveloc's career in Constantine's reign depends.[19] The chronology and the British succession derive from the *Historia regum Britanniae*, a work only recently appeared when Gaimar was composing his own history. Sufficient time cannot possibly have elapsed between the appearance of the *Historia* and Gaimar's acquisition of the Danish materials for Galfridian elements to have found their way into the Haveloc story. Prior to the *Estoire des Engleis* the tale probably defied precise chronological positioning within the framework of Insular history. If anything, there would be a natural tendency to associate the Danes with a much later period.

The Haveloc story bears all the marks of being an interpolation made when the composition had reached a fairly advanced stage. Bell has adduced linguistic evidence which suggests that Gaimar had proceeded some distance with the *Estoire des Engleis* before inserting certain of the Danish episodes.[20] The implications are extremely interesting. Haveloc's career culminates in the formation of a conjoint Dano-British realm, and the importance attached to

Adelbrit's and Edelsi's kingdoms in the tale undoubtedly antedates the *Estoire des Engleis*. But it was Gaimar who saw in the post-Arthurian era the necessary degree of political instability to permit incorporation of the story. In other words, Constantine's reign offered an appropriate juncture to make the interpolation because Gaimar already perceived the mid-sixth century as a time of political fragmentation. In fact, the characterization of Constantine's reign falls before, not after, the Gildas reference. It is in the prologue to the *Estoire des Engleis* that the political situation is sketched and a larger historical context provided for the events to follow.

The principal source for the *Estoire des Engleis* is the *Anglo-Saxon Chronicle*. The prologue mediates between Geoffrey of Monmouth's depiction of the sixth century and that offered by English annalists. Constantine does not appear in the *Chronicle*; indeed, the entries for the period in question contain very little information of any kind on the Britons. There certainly is no indication of Danish involvement in Insular affairs at so early a date. Nevertheless, Gaimar's perception of the era as a time of political division and interracial struggle – an age which witnessed the emergence of the English and their gradual expansion – derives from the *Anglo-Saxon Chronicle*. Gaimar uses a Galfridian device, Modred's Donation, to effect a transition between two radically different views of the sixth century. The turbulence does, to be sure, afford him an opportunity to press the Danish claim through the Haveloc story, but in all likelihood he had already altered the character of Constantine's reign in preparation for paraphrasing the *Anglo-Saxon Chronicle*.

The significant differences between the *Estoire des Engleis* and the *Historia regum Britanniae* strongly suggest that Gaimar did not follow the outlines of the Galfridian construct beyond Arthur's demise. I cannot believe that Geffrei Gaimar depicted Constantine's reign twice in two radically different fashions. It is illogical to suppose that in the lost portion of the text Gaimar followed Geoffrey in laying Modred's Donation to rest only to resurrect the matter at the opening of the *Estoire des Engleis*. Constantine's troubled reign is treated in the context of English history because the territorial concessions made by Arthur's nephew would prove the key factor in the Anglo-Saxon conquest of Britain. Much later in the account, Cnut reminds Edmund Ironside of the unholy alliance which provided the English with a base for their expansion (EdE, lines 4301–18, p 137). Geffrei Gaimar has many weaknesses, but a lack of thematic continuity is not one of them. I am persuaded that Gaimar abandoned the *Historia regum Britanniae* following Arthur's departure for Avalon, and then effected a transition not only to the chronological framework of the *Anglo-Saxon Chronicle*, but to the entire image of the sixth century found therein.

By placing the dividing line right after the Battle of Camlann, Gaimar would seem to have contrasted the strong centralized government of Arthur's reign with the fragmentation which followed. The turmoil of the mid-sixth century is attributed to the fact that each of the competing interests possessed a portion of the heartlands. Gaimar treats these territorial divisions as the hallmark of a transitional period and does not regard fragmented rule as a mode of governance characteristic of one particular ethnic group. Following the Haveloc story, the *Estoire des Engleis* draws heavily on the *Anglo-Saxon Chronicle*, and several English kingdoms figure in the account. Gaimar, however, depicts the Germanic conquest of Britain as essentially a West Saxon achievement. He picks up the chronology in the *Anglo-Saxon Chronicle* with the arrival of Cerdic (EDE, lines 817–24, p 25. Cf ASC p 11) and traces the emergence of Wessex as the dominant force in English history. The importance of the West Saxons quickly becomes evident. It is Cynric who drives the Britons back beyond the Severn and conquers the Danish lands (EDE, lines 853–920, pp 26–8). Gaimar's account appears to move from the centralized rule of Arthur's day across a lengthy period of strife to West Saxon domination and another era of unified rule. The parallels with Geoffrey's own view of developments down to the tenth century are striking, but Gaimar does not denigrate Anglo-Saxon achievement in the interim.

Geffrei Gaimar's depiction of sixth-century Britain bespeaks an awareness of at least one major point on which Geoffrey of Monmouth was at variance with standard authorities. The handling of materials in the *Estoire des Engleis* can hardly be considered a vindication of contemporary historical methods, but a critical attitude toward the *Historia* is very much in evidence. Gaimar used available controlling data to evaluate Geoffrey's testimony, and gave precedence to the prior authority of the *Anglo-Saxon Chronicle*. The reference to Gildas at the start of the Haveloc story further indicates a clear perception of the basic issues and conflicts. Gaimar fully comprehends the incompatibility of the Galfridian and Anglo-Saxon viewpoints. For this reason the passage of dominion defines the limits of Geoffrey's usability. Because of the Danish claim, the periodization in the *Estoire des Engleis* remains unique, but Gaimar's sense that the *Historia* had to be abandoned after the passing of British rule is also a feature of the next account to be considered.

At approximately the same time as Gaimar completed the *Estoire des Engleis*, Alfred of Beverley embarked upon his *Annales*.[21] The work is the earliest surviving example of the incorporation of a substantial portion of the *Historia regum Britanniae* into an overview of Insular history. Alfred's treatment of the pre-Saxon era makes up half of the account (Books 1–5). Geoffrey's regnal list provides the underlying framework, but Alfred adheres to the

Historia only down through the reign of Keredic. Gormund's invasion is depicted as triggering those events which brought the end of British rule.

Alfred of Beverley exploits the fact that Geoffrey depicts two occasions on which Loegria was wrested from the Britons. The first occurs when Gormund hands the British heartlands over to the Saxons (HRB, c 186, p 282); the second, when Germanic settlers overrun Loegria following the plague in Cadwaladr's lifetime (HRB, c 204, p 301). Of these two, the first immediately precedes Augustine's mission. Alfred identifies Gormund's campaign as the decisive loss of territorial control, thereby fixing the passage of dominion prior to events which Bede assigned to English history.

The overriding importance of reconciling the periodization with Bede is clear as Alfred draws the era of British rule to a close. Following the account of Gormund's depredations, the lamentable state of Insular Christianity is described (AB, p 74; HRB, c 186, pp 282–3). Alfred then inserts what purports to be corroborating testimony from Bede (AB, pp 74–5; HE, 1.15, p 52). The passage in question, however, refers to the unholy alliance between the Picts and the Saxons in the fifth century, not long after the arrival of Hengist and Horsa (HE, 1.15, pp 48–50). By means of this pact, divine retribution is said to have been visited on the Britons. Alfred begins the quotation so as to obliterate the original context, and then applies Bede's general statement on the rise of the pagans and the decline of the Britons to a later point in time. The passage fits the circumstances, not the chronology. Alfred is attempting to mediate between Geoffrey and Bede, and resorts to a highly dubious expedient.

After citing Bede, Alfred returns to the *Historia regum Britanniae* and borrows Geoffrey's comment on the Britons' loss of sovereignty in the wake of Gormund's campaign: 'Amiserunt itaque regni diadema Britones et insulæ monarchiam, nec pristinam dignitatem deinceps recuperare potuerunt' (AB, p 75; HRB, c 187, p 283). The renaming of the Britons immediately follows as Alfred moves up Galfridian materials found at the very end of the *Historia* (HRB, c 207, p 303).[22] According to Geoffrey, Gormund drove both Keredic and bands of British survivors into Wales (HRB, cc 184–6, pp 281–2). Alfred seems to have regarded the situation as justifying insertion of the name change at this juncture. Two discrete occurrences from Geoffrey's *Historia* are interrelated causally. Alfred's handling of the materials fixes the loss of dominion with considerable precision and permits a sharp demarcation between eras.

Before concluding Book 5, Alfred inserts a close paraphrase of yet another passage from the *Historia ecclesiastica* (AB, pp 75–6; HE, 1.14, p 48). Bede is describing the plight of the Britons in the period between the appeal to Aetius (HE, 1.13, p 46) and the initial Saxon landings (HE, 1.15, pp 48–50). Henry of Huntingdon ends Book 1 of the *Historia Anglorum* in like fashion (HA, 1.47, pp

36–7). Alfred knew Henry's work and appears to be using it as a model at this point. The passage in question, however, fits chronologically into the *Historia Anglorum*, but not into the *Annales*. Alfred applies the statement to events more than a century after the arrival of Hengist and Horsa. The chronological displacement seems a consequence of Alfred's efforts to reconcile his principal sources before proceeding. The material from Bede is then merged with Geoffrey's statement regarding the Saxons' prudent behaviour in rebuilding Britain (AB, p 76; HRB, c 207, p 303). The passage omits any reference to Athelstan probably due to the dates of his reign.

Having followed Geoffrey down into the last quarter of the sixth century, Alfred now attempts to mark the passage of dominion by means of the Heptarchy. In Alfred's view the dividing line between the two eras must fall before the start of Augustine's mission in 597. Because of the emphasis on centralized government in the *Historia regum Britanniae*, Henry of Huntingdon's identification of early English rule with the Heptarchy provides Alfred with a convenient marker, but the chronology has become problematic. Whereas Henry had traced the evolution of this mode of governance beginning with Hengist and Horsa, Alfred adhered to Geoffrey of Monmouth's account down to a point immediately preceding Augustine's arrival. Gormund's campaign is the proximate cause of this mission, and to make matters worse, the emergence of the Anglo-Saxon kingdoms is not treated at all in Geoffrey's depiction. Alfred of Beverley has the Heptarchy at his disposal to herald the advent of a new era, but no room in the chronology to indicate the gradual development of the kingdoms.

Thanks to Gormund's Donation, Alfred does not need to portray the role of the Germanic enclaves in the piecemeal conquest of Britain. He requires only an institutional manifestation of the passage of dominion, and the problem is resolved by a simple expedient. Alfred adapts a description of the English kingdoms for use as a chronological indicator. Book 6 of the *Annales* opens with a sketch of the Heptarchy which rests on the prefatory list of early kingdoms in the *Historia Anglorum* (AB, pp 77–8; HA, 1.4, pp 8–9). Whereas Henry of Huntingdon separates this description from the account proper, Alfred incorporates the materials into the systematic record of events. The enormous compression of Henry's list provides a sharp division.

Alfred of Beverley uses Henry's list of kingdoms to mark the advent of Anglo-Saxon rule. The new era begins when the Angles 'de uno regno Britanniæ septem regna constituerunt' (AB, p 77). The partitioning of a previously unified land becomes the institutional manifestation of a change in the ethnic background of Britain's rulers. Geoffrey's association of the Britons with centralized government has clearly reinforced the usefulness of the Heptarchy.

Each kingdom is enumerated together with its principal cities and first rulers (AB, pp 77–8). Alfred supplies data appropriate to the list's new function in a chronological survey. Leaving aside minor changes in the cities mentioned, information is added on the first kings of the seven realms. The foundings of Kent, Sussex, and Wessex are actually dated. Whereas Henry of Huntingdon restricted himself to descriptive items, Alfred includes material bearing on the chronological placement of the kingdoms. The supplemental data are gleaned from those later entries in the *Historia Anglorum* where the individual found-ings are discussed. The selection is governed by the list's function, and there can be no doubt that Alfred was aware of the rather different requirements of his usage.

Alfred's sketch of the Heptarchy compresses events which spanned a con-siderable period of time. He had no intention of rehearsing the histories of the several kingdoms, because to do so would render the Heptarchy unusable for precise periodization. For this reason, certain aspects of the chronology are left vague. Despite the addition of historical detail, Alfred makes it impossible to reconstruct the actual events. The order of Henry's list is retained, even though it is at variance with the chronological sequence of the foundings.[23] Alfred collects data from the subsequent entries in the *Historia Anglorum* and might have been expected to catch such a discrepancy. The order of the kingdoms provides a preliminary indication that matters of detailed chronology are not to be given precedence. Alfred's usage requires both the semblance of a historical survey and the obfuscation of certain realities.

Alfred avoids calling attention to the duration of time required for the emergence of the kingdoms. This consideration would seem to underlie the selective use of dating materials available in the *Historia Anglorum*. Alfred follows Henry in placing the foundings of Kent, Sussex, and Wessex relative to the arrival of Hengist and Horsa. These three kingdoms are said to have been established eight years (AB, p 77; HA, 2.4, p 41), thirty years (AB, p 77; HA, 2.8, p 44), and seventy-one years (AB, p 78; HA, 2.16, p 47) after the initial landing respectively. Unlike his source, however, Alfred never gives the year in which Hengist and Horsa arrived (cf HA, 2.1, p 38). Geoffrey of Monmouth also does not supply the date, and Alfred is following the *Historia regum Britanniae* at the time the landing is described (AB, p 49; HRB, c 98, p 175). The omission may be a simple oversight, but one important change is made in the Galfridian version of this event. Alfred reintroduces Vortigern's invitation, borrowing material verbatim from Bede (HE, 1.14, p 48). In the *Historia ecclesiastica* this passage brings the chapter to a close, but the opening sentence of the next section dates the arrival of the Germanic invaders in 449 (HE, 1.15, p 48). There can be no doubting how well Alfred knew the *Historia ecclesiastica*; indeed, he cites Bede's famous description of the landings at a later point, again without the date (AB, p 78). Although Alfred's motives cannot be inferred with complete certainty, I find it difficult to believe that the omission of such a famous date – readily available both in Bede and Henry of Huntingdon – is fortuitous. It suits Alfred's purpose admirably that the precise date of the arrival of Hengist and Horsa be shrouded in vagueness. The Galfridian construct appears to have been irreconcileable with Anglo-Saxon tradition.

Alfred also exhibits a certain reluctance to provide dating poles between which events can be ranged. Henry assigns the founding of Wessex and Northumbria to specific years, 519 and 547 respectively (HA, 2.16, p 47; 2.21, p 50). Alfred supplies a date only for Wessex and emphasizes this kingdom's long-term importance to English history (AB, p 78). As with the other information provided, the value of this specific item is more apparent than real. The inclusion of one date draws notice to a particular kingdom, but two dates would permit the ordering and locating of what lies between. Alfred does not want even an approximate chronology of events. The only comment regarding the time spanned by the foundings involves the arrivals of the first rulers. Alfred observes simply: 'Omnes autem isti septem reges fuerunt pagani, sed non omnes simul in Britanniam venerunt' (AB, p 78). Such cavalier treatment of chronological detail is noteworthy and probably purposeful.

Having alluded to the Germanic invasions, Alfred backs up to a time before the emergence of the Heptarchy. Bede's famous description of the incursions by the Angles, the Saxons, and the Jutes is inserted at this juncture (AB, p 78; HE, 1.15, p 50). Because the foundings of the several kingdoms depend upon the influx of Germanic peoples, the passage is obviously out of sequence. That would appear to be the reason for omitting the date. Alfred then recounts how, as the years went by, the invaders flourished, and the island was renamed after the Angles: 'Sicut enim insula, quæ quondam cum a gigantibus incoleretur Albion dicebatur, postea expulsis, fugatisque, et occisis gigantibus a Bruto Britannia vocata est, ita tercio loco ab Anglis Anglia nominatur' (AB, p 78). Alfred now returns to Bede's account of the invasions and adds information on Hengist and Horsa, tracing their descent back to Woden (AB, pp 78–9; HE, 1.15, p 50). Brief mention is made of the fact that the Anglo-Saxon kingdoms vied amongst themselves for supremacy, but the comment is very vague: 'In primordio enim regni Anglorum non unum erat inter eos regnum, sed, ut quæque provincia potencior erat, proprium sibi regem constituebat' (AB, p 79). This situation is said to have continued until the reign of Athelstan, the first English king to rule over the entire island. The first Christian sovereigns among the Anglo-Saxons are then enumerated as Alfred effects a transition to the kingdom of Kent under Æthelberht (AB, p 79).

In the *Annales* the running account of Anglo-Saxon history begins with the accession of Æthelberht to the throne of Kent (AB, p 79). The arrangement of materials implies that the Heptarchy took shape prior to this juncture. Yet according to Henry of Huntingdon, both East Anglia and Mercia were founded after Æthelberht's accession.[24] Because Alfred draws his information on the first East Anglian and Mercian kings from the relevant entries in the *Historia Anglorum*, it must be assumed that he was aware of the difficulty.

Alfred of Beverley dates the accession of Æthelberht in the year 560. As William of Malmesbury points out, there is a five-year discrepancy between Bede and the *Anglo-Saxon Chronicle* on this point (GRA, 1.9, 1:13). The existence of these two traditions reveals a shift in the *Annales*. Alfred is now following Bede exclusively (HE, 2.5, p 148). Henry of Huntingdon dates Æthelberht's accession five years later (HA, 2.23, p 51). Alfred has availed himself of Henry's description of the Heptarchy in order to effect a transition to the *Historia ecclesiastica*.

What underlies the recurrent intrusion of materials from Bede at the start of Book 6 is now clear. The means of marking the passage of dominion derive from Henry of Huntingdon, but Alfred is attempting to reconcile his periodization with the *Historia ecclesiastica*. He has inserted the Heptarchy between Geoffrey's British materials and those events which, on the authority of Bede, must be assigned to Anglo-Saxon history. Alfred is reconciling not Henry but Geoffrey with the *Historia ecclesiastica*. Throughout the *Annales* Bede serves as the principal control on the *Historia regum Britanniae*, and this interrelationship, so fundamental to Alfred's account, dictates the abandonment of Geoffrey immediately following the reign of Keredic.[25]

On numerous occasions in the depiction of the pre-Saxon era Alfred of Beverley exhibits a marked preference for the testimony of Bede.[26] The periodization is consistent with this earlier usage. It is because of Bede, and not Henry of Huntingdon, that Alfred perceives a need to shift the focus of the account prior to Augustine's arrival. The use made of the Heptarchy implies that Anglo-Saxon rule has assumed its identifying form by 560. This notion is totally without basis in the chronology of the *Historia Anglorum*, where the founding of both East Anglia and Mercia falls after the accession of Æthelberht. Alfred's concern is with the character of temporal rule, but on Bede's authority he begins the running account of the Anglo-Saxon era with an event crucial to subsequent ecclesiastical history. Æthelberht's reign is important to the future of Insular Christianity, not to the political map of England. Alfred employs the Heptarchy as a marker, but there can be little doubt as to his reasons for placing the dividing line where he does.

Alfred mediates between two accounts in which the nascent English kingdoms do not figure prominently. Both Geoffrey and Bede acknowledge the existence of political divisions among the Anglo-Saxons, but the early kingdoms have no distinct time slot, such as is found in Henry of Huntingdon. Because of Geoffrey's emphasis on unified rule, the fragmentation of the Anglo-Saxons remains a useful identifying feature of their dominion. The problem is one of accommodating the Heptarchy chronologically. Geoffrey of Monmouth fills the first hundred years and more of the Anglo-Saxon presence with a compelling narrative of British affairs. Bede's authority establishes a *terminus ante quem* for the start of English history, but Alfred must scramble up essential details omitted earlier by Geoffrey. If the *Historia regum Britanniae* is followed down through the reign of Keredic, then a writer must choose between an awkward transition and loss of the early Anglo-Saxon kingdoms.

Just how precarious the position of the Heptarchy really was can be seen from the conflate manuscript of the *Historia regum Britanniae* and the *Historia Anglorum*, housed at Ushaw College, Durham.[27] Through the physical union of two texts the anonymous compiler produces a coherent overview of Insular history. Geoffrey of Monmouth provides the material on the Britons, Henry of Huntingdon the Anglo-Saxon and Anglo-Norman data. The manuscript belongs to the second half of the twelfth century, and the periodization illustrates precisely what Alfred of Beverley sought to avoid.

The conjoining of the *Historia regum Britanniae* and the *Historia Anglorum* is handled in mechanical fashion. The compiler breaks off Geoffrey's account with the description of the aftermath of Gormund's Donation (HRB, c 187, p 283). The final sentence is the one which immediately precedes the report of Augustine's arrival. The subsequent quires were then dropped and replaced by Henry of Huntingdon's depiction of events from Augustine's mission down to the year 1139. The missing quires from Geoffrey's history were not discarded but rather were bound in at the end of the volume.

Henry of Huntingdon takes up Augustine's mission in Book 3 of the *Historia Anglorum*. Book 1 is devoted to pre-Saxon history. The later compiler substitutes Geoffrey's account of the Britons down to 597 and then dovetails the two chronologies. By so doing, he loses the materials covered in Book 2 of the *Historia Anglorum* where Henry chronicles the emergence of the Heptarchy. Alfred of Beverley uses the same periodization but preserves at least the substance of Henry's Book 2 by including a sketch of the English kingdoms. Alfred is motivated by the desire to have an institutional marker for the passage of dominion and undoubtedly realized that a strictly chronological arrangement would obliterate the principal identifying feature of early Anglo-Saxon rule.

The second half of the twelfth century does not offer a wealth of material for tracing the response to Geoffrey's periodization in the context of a systematic overview of Insular history. Right around 1200, however, Gervase of Canterbury attests to the continuing struggle with the transition from British to Anglo-Saxon rule.[28] His *Gesta regum* sketches the outlines of Britain's past from the birth of Brutus onwards. The account is enormously compressed with Geoffrey's regnal list serving as the framework for the first part of the depiction.

The outlines of the *Historia regum Britanniae* are followed down to Gormund's Donation and the flight of the surviving Britons: 'Amiserunt itaque Britones regni diadema multis temporibus et insulæ monarchiam. Careticus autem fugit in Gualliam et deinceps non comparuit' (GC, 2:19–20). At this juncture Gervase inserts Chapter 22 of Book 1 of Bede's *Historia ecclesiastica* in its entirety (GC, 2:20; HE, 1.22, pp 66–8). The passage in question is where Bede resumes his discussion of the aftermath of Mount Badon, having interrupted the chronological flow to recount the activities of St Germanus. In the *Historia ecclesiastica* this chapter provides a transition from the British triumph at Mount Badon to the background for Augustine's mission. The decline of the Britons is described in the vaguest of terms and attributed to sins which 'Gildas flebili sermone describit' (HE, 1.22, p 68).

Whereas Bede had no events with which he might trace the British fall, Gervase did. In the *Gesta regum* the passage from the *Historia ecclesiastica* has become not a substitute for information regarding the activities of the Britons in the sixth century, but a recapitulation of the developments from Arthur to Keredic. The gap in the *Historia ecclesiastica* has been filled with Galfridian materials which fit the resurgence-decline pattern sketched by Bede. Unlike Alfred of Beverley, who could only correlate the *Historia ecclesiastica* with the *Historia regum Britanniae* by citing Bede out of context, Gervase of Canterbury seized a fairly obvious point of congruence between the two works.

Gervase does not correlate the sources in preparation for abandoning the *Historia regum Britanniae*. The précis of Geoffrey's account resumes with Augustine's mission. Gervase omits the negative characterization of the conversion effort but refrains from substituting an alternative depiction, even though one lay close at hand in Bede's *Historia ecclesiastica*. Geoffrey's version of events is merely stripped of its British bias, leaving little more than the fact of the mission: 'Erat autem tunc temporis Ethelbertus rex in Cantia potentissimus; Ethelfridus vero in Northumbria; et tunc venit in Angliam Sanctus Augustinus, prædicandi gratia a beato papa Gregorio missus' (GC, 2:20). Gervase makes no effort whatsoever to define Augustine's historical significance, a surprising decision for a man whose life and works were centred around Christ

Church in Canterbury.[29] The *Gesta regum* remains an epitome of Geoffrey's *Historia* and not a compilation of available sources. Chapter 22 of Book 1 of the *Historia ecclesiastica* is the only non-Galfridian material included, and this single interpolation can hardly be said to alter the epitomist character of the depiction. Gervase seems willing to omit selected data throughout, but rather loath to add information, even from Bede. The *Gesta regum* is the product of a more reverential attitude toward Geoffrey of Monmouth than has been seen thus far.[30]

Gervase of Canterbury follows the contours of Geoffrey's *Historia* down through Cadwaladr's reign. He recounts the famine which ravaged the island forcing the British sovereign and large numbers of his subjects to flee. As a result, the island fell victim to large-scale Saxon invasions: 'Præterea tot Saxonum nationes et viri concupiscentes aliena in Britanniam advenerunt post Hengistum et Horsum, ut regnum Britanniæ in septem partes dividerent, et nomens ibi regium usurparent' (GC, 2:21). The date of Cadwaladr's death is not supplied, but Gervase has obviously placed the formation of the Heptarchy at the very end of the seventh century. The names of the kingdoms are now listed, and Gervase cites the emergence of this form of government as the reason for changing the island's name: 'Deletum est itaque nomen Britanniæ, et ab Anglis Anglia nuncupatur' (GC, 2:21). Having introduced the traditional institutional marker, Gervase takes up the origins of the Germanic peoples. The Britons have been seen to descend from Aeneas, and he will now trace the lineage of early English kings back to Woden (GC, 2:21–2). The histories of the various realms are then discussed individually, before returning to a chronological arrangement of the data.

Gervase's handling of the post-Arthurian segment of the *Historia regum Britanniae* does not bespeak an acute awareness of the fundamental conflict between the Galfridian and Anglo-Saxon perspectives. Despite firsthand knowledge of Bede's depiction, no hard decisions on Geoffrey's reliability were deemed necessary. Gervase simply does not use the available English authorities as a control on the *Historia*. The contrast with Geffrei Gaimar and Alfred of Beverley is striking. For these earlier writers the passage of dominion defined the limits of Geoffrey's usability. Once the end of British rule had been marked, the *Historia* was felt to be no longer compatible with Anglo-Saxon tradition, and both men abandoned the Galfridian construct well before the end. Gervase, on the other hand, notes the passing of British dominion but then follows Geoffrey's account through to Cadwaladr's demise.

Before discussing the individual kingdoms of the Heptarchy, Gervase signals the fundamental importance of William of Malmesbury's *Gesta regum Anglorum* for matters pertaining to English history. Whoever desires information on the Britons should consult Geoffrey of Monmouth, while William is the preferred authority for the Anglo-Saxons (GC, 2:23). Gervase heeds his own advice. Just as he relied on Geoffrey for data on the Britons, so now much of his information on subsequent developments will be drawn from William of Malmesbury. The fact that the *Historia regum Britanniae* overlaps with the *Gesta regum Anglorum* for a considerable space does not prompt an effort to correlate the depictions. Gervase seems to regard Geoffrey and William as incontrovertible authorities for two distinct strands of Insular history. In essence, British and Anglo-Saxon rule are treated as separate subjects, and laid end to end.

Gervase of Canterbury and William of Newburgh were contemporaries. If the question is posed as to which of these two men in his attitude toward the *Historia regum Britanniae* represented the general trend around 1200, then the answer must be Gervase. The depth of William's concern and the entire thrust of his denunciation become understandable when viewed in light of Gervase's *Gesta regum*.

It has often been remarked that William of Newburgh's discussion of Gildas, Bede, and Geoffrey of Monmouth is curiously out of place in a history which begins with the Norman Conquest. Determining the weight to be assigned testimony from these three sources has no bearing whatsoever on the compilation of the *Historia rerum Anglicarum*. William in fact states that, thanks to the efforts of writers who came after Bede, the entire course of Insular history need not be rehearsed (HRA, 1:18–19). These chroniclers remain unnamed, but presumably they gave precedence to venerable authority in a manner consonant with William's own views. He knew and used Henry of Huntingdon's *Historia Anglorum* (Gransden, p 264), a work which does indeed draw heavily on Bede, as do most pre-Galfridian surveys. The years which separated William of Newburgh from Henry's generation of systematizers had produced mostly chronicles of contemporary or near-contemporary events. Others had shared William's conviction that the depiction and analysis of developments in the post-Conquest era constituted a more pressing desideratum than renewed attempts to understand the distant past.

But William's lifetime also witnessed a revival of interest in large-scale, comprehensive surveys. One hallmark of these works was a generally uncritical attitude toward Geoffrey of Monmouth. As Partner observes, William of Newburgh 'seems to be arguing with some other body of opinion' (Partner, p 62), and I believe that his disquisition on the sources of early Insular history was prompted by the current practices of men like Gervase of Canterbury. At the close of the century the *Historia regum Britanniae* would hardly have struck any well-informed historian as new and shocking; yet William's denunciation carries something of the indignation normally associated with recent discoveries. It is the kind of scathing attack which might have been expected right after Geoffrey's account appeared. What *was* new around 1200 was not the Galfridian construct, but the weight assigned to its testimony. And William focuses his attack on this very point.

There is nothing to suggest that William of Newburgh knew the works of Alfred of Beverley and Geffrei Gaimar. Consequently, a direct comparison with the methods of earlier writers who made extensive use of Geoffrey's *Historia* cannot have motivated William. I rather doubt that he would have approved of their solutions anyway. More likely, he looked back to Henry of Huntingdon across a half-century of Geoffrey's virtual exclusion from the works of major historians. The intervening years had brought chronicles of recent events in which William would have found little more than scattered allusions to Arthur and to the vaticinations of Merlin. The pattern of inclusions in these histories and in the twelfth century generally can be misleading. William of Newburgh may have concluded that, despite the Arthurian mania, the *Historia regum Britanniae* was safely relegated to the realm of popular literature and dynastic propaganda. Though hardly desirable, the level of intrusion into serious history-writing would not have seemed to imperil what Bede and others had wrought. If William did form an initial judgment on the basis of observable usage, then one can understand his concern at discovering that the entire question of Geoffrey's credibility had never been resolved. In William's day the *Historia regum Britanniae* actually posed a far greater threat to the foundations of Insular historiography than at any other time since its appearance.

William of Newburgh may well be our most important witness to a basic feature of Geoffrey of Monmouth's reception in the twelfth century. Issues of a very fundamental nature were left lying by those writers who first grappled with the *Historia*. Nor did the initial enthusiasm give way to greater rigour in evaluating Geoffrey's testimony. Around mid-century the major talents may have turned their attentions elsewhere, but the *Historia regum Britanniae* did not need their citations to become history. The text itself was regarded as factual, and by William of Newburgh's day, when contemporary historians once again took up the remote past, fifty years of general acceptance can be seen to have had its effect. Writers like Gervase of Canterbury seem to have lost all sense of the fundamental conflict between the Galfridian and Anglo-Saxon views of sixth- and seventh-century Insular history. With the passage of time Geoffrey of Monmouth and William of Malmesbury had come to be placed on a par with each other, even though the underpinnings of their respective accounts were so very different. Gervase and his entire generation no longer perceived the Galfridian construct as a challenge to prevailing notions. They were simply too far from the work's appearance for that, and chronological remove tended to have a levelling effect on the weight of individual testimony. William of Newburgh placed such heavy emphasis on Gildas and Bede in an effort to reawaken an awareness of the basic issues and contradictions. But William responded to observable trends, and when the drift had become clear, it was already too late.

At the close of the century compendious surveys devoted exclusively to Britain's past remain rare. Contemporary and near-contemporary affairs attract a great deal of attention, but concern for the broad sweeps of history is nonetheless very much in evidence. Rather than concentrating on Insular developments to the extent found in William of Malmesbury and Henry of Huntingdon, Ralph Diceto and Roger of Wendover set themselves the task of correlating the overview produced by these men and their successors with the outlines of universal history. Robert of Torigni had declined to incorporate Geoffrey's *Historia* into his chronicle, and, although Ralph Diceto's handling of Geoffrey is very similar, the gradual intrusion of Galfridian data into the two principal manuscripts of the *Abbreviationes chronicorum* does reveal a trend. Universal chronicles would be the last type of historical writing to receive Geoffrey of Monmouth, and this development marks an important stage in the reception of the *Historia*.

At the start of the *Abbreviationes chronicorum*, a work which covers the period from the Creation to 1148, Ralph Diceto lists forty-seven authorities for his depiction, but Geoffrey's name does not appear among them (RD, 1:20–3). Ralph held Robert of Torigni in evident high esteem, and it does not seem unreasonable to suggest that this precedent influenced the exclusion of Geoffrey of Monmouth from the *Abbreviationes*. Elsewhere in Ralph's historical writings there is ample evidence that he harboured no distrust of the *Historia regum Britanniae*. In the *Ymagines historiarum*, a chronicle of recent events which begins where the *Abbreviationes* end (1148), several events are regarded as fulfilling Merlin's prophecies.[31] Moreover, Ralph made a separate abstract of Geoffrey's *Historia* very much in the tradition of Henry of Huntingdon's epistolary summary (RD, 2:222–32). On balance I am inclined to think that Ralph Diceto consciously followed Robert of Torigni's lead.

Stubbs' edition of the *Abbreviationes* is based on the A-text (Lambeth ms 8) which was 'no doubt an original possession of the author, and must by him have been left among the archives of his cathedral' (RD, 1: lxxxix). Ralph lived at St Paul's, London, and the B-text would also seem to have been produced at this location.[32] As can be seen from the interpolations, the compiler of B had access to the same sources and elaborated a variety of specific points throughout the account. Although Geoffrey of Monmouth's name is omittted from the list of authorities, the A-text does contain some Galfridian data.[33] Additional materials from the *Historia* have been added to the B-text.[34] Irrespective of how the items came to be included, Geoffrey of Monmouth has begun to make himself felt in the compilation of universal histories. In both texts of the *Abbreviationes* the periodization remains essentially pre-Galfridian. Not enough data were included to force a reassessment of the Britons' position, but this would soon change.

It was Roger of Wendover who first integrated the Galfridian construct with universal history.[35] St Albans' importance for historical writing in thirteenth-century England hardly needs to be emphasized, but Roger's role in the reception of the *Historia regum Britanniae* has not received sufficient attention. The *Flores historiarum* treat events from the Creation to 1202, and Geoffrey of Monmouth is given equal status among the authorities used in the compilation. Roger's work marks the full-scale entry of Galfridian materials into a branch of historical writing from which these data had been virtually excluded for a half-century and more. The *Flores historiarum* provided a foundation for Matthew Paris, thereby ensuring that Roger's handling of Geoffrey would be an influential model for succeeding generations.

From the outset Roger simply correlates the *Historia* with his other sources.[36] The compilation is so broad in scope that the regular insertion of Galfridian sections does not seriously distort the familiar contours of universal history. The data do, of course, convey a sense of the Britons' importance to this larger context, but Roger selects and compresses the material from the *Historia*, avoiding any obvious quantitative imbalance. With the arrival of Hengist and Horsa the mode of composition does not change. Roger interweaves both the Galfridian and the Anglo-Saxon versions of events with the various other strands of history. The rise of the house of Constantine and even the reign of Arthur are broken up to permit insertion of entries on a wide range of historical topics, including the Anglo-Saxon kingdoms. For example, notice of Cerdic's death immediately precedes Arthur's conquest of Norway and Denmark. There then follow three entries bearing on religious history, before Roger takes up Modred's appointment as co-regent and King Arthur's final Continental campaign (RW, 1:70–1). The account in the *Flores historiarum* disrupts the flow of Geoffrey's narrative, leaving little trace of the momentum which builds in the *Historia* prior to Arthur's reign.

Roger's handling of the passage of dominion is highly original. Information has been provided on the Anglo-Saxon kingdoms since the arrival of Hengist and Horsa, and right before Keredic's accession Roger pauses to list the realms

(RW, 1:88–9). The reason for emphasizing the kingdoms at this juncture becomes clear when Roger completely eliminates Gormund from the account. The Anglo-Saxon rulers themselves rise up against Keredic and drive the Britons into the more remote regions of the island. Roger conceives of the period between 449 and this rebellion as a time of British domination during which the English kingdoms were established. By Keredic's day the Anglo-Saxon enclaves had gained sufficient power and stability to throw off the British yoke. Roger has combined the Galfridian version of events with the older notion that the English kingdoms provided a framework for the conquest of Britain. Such a correlation presupposes the roughly eqivalent weight of the two viewpoints. To be sure, English reliance on Gormund's military might has become incompatible with the depiction of the emergent kingdoms, but with this single exception, Roger integrates the Galfridian and Anglo-Saxon perspectives, heedless of the inherent contradictions.

By eliminating Gormund's Donation, Roger removes the stigma attached to receiving control of the heartlands from the hands of a foreign conqueror. The motivation for the rebellion remains Galfridian, but credit for the take-over has been returned to the Anglo-Saxons. Roger also retains Geoffrey's account of the depredations and particularly the razing of churches which accompanied the campaign against Keredic. The responsibility must now be borne by the English kings, and Roger comments on their pagan barbarism (RW, 1:89–90). Geoffrey's comment on the Britons' loss of sovereignty is now added: 'Itaque Britanni regni diadema multis temporibus amittentes, videlicet usque ad tempora Cadwallonis, quem Beda Cedwallam vocat, illam patriæ partem, quæ eis remanserat, non uni regi sed tribus tyrannis subjectam, civilibus bellis sæpissime infestare non cessabant' (RW, 1:90–1). The three kingdoms are identified as Cornwall, Demetia, and Venedotia. Roger then traces the enmity between the Welsh and the English in his own day back to the situation at the close of the sixth century. As if to underscore the importance of the enclaves, a second discussion of the Anglo-Saxon kingdoms is inserted at this point, followed by notice of the island's renaming: 'His ita dispositis, placuit dictis regibus Britanniam et memoriam Britannorum penitus delere; unde communiter statuerunt quatenus insula, non a Bruto Britannia, sed Anglia vocaretur' (RW, 1:92–3).

For a time hereafter Roger of Wendover gives precedence to Anglo-Saxon tradition, but beginning with Cadwallon and Edwin (RW, 1:130–1), he once again includes substantial amounts of material from the *Historia*. Geoffrey's account is correlated with the other sources down through the end of Cadwaladr's reign. At this point Roger remarks the end of the *Historia regum*

Britanniae and even quotes the epilogue in which Geoffrey leaves subsequent events to Caradog of Llancarfan, William of Malmesbury, and Henry of Huntingdon (RW, 1:184).

By the turn of the century writers have begun to approach Galfridian history in a manner far different from their predecessors fifty or sixty years earlier. The abruptness with which a new reverence manifests itself in Gervase of Canterbury is undoubtedly due to the distribution of the historiographic witnesses. This attitude toward Geoffrey's *Historia* must have evolved gradually, and the pace was probably far from uniform. But that does not make the change any less striking. Although Geffrei Gaimar and Alfred of Beverley fell easy prey to King Arthur's appeal, they evince an acute sense of the problems inherent in Geoffrey's depiction of the sixth and seventh centuries. Their handling of the post-Arthurian era bespeaks a shared conviction that this segment of the *Historia* was incompatible with Anglo-Saxon tradition. Each abandons the Galfridian frame at a point which coincides with the passage of dominion. A simple shift in emphasis, that is, giving precedence to English authorities while continuing to insert Galfridian data, apparently did not strike Geffrei Gaimar and Alfred of Beverley as a feasible alternative. To their way of thinking, this was no more possible than charting the emergence of the Anglo-Saxon kingdoms in the midst of Arthur's reign. By about 1200, however, the two versions of Insular developments had ceased to be regarded as mutually exclusive. Placement of the passage of dominion in Keredic's reign has become conventional, but gone is the sense that the *Historia* could not be followed beyond this point.

Although the various stations remain obscure, Geoffrey of Monmouth became an acknowledged authority somewhere around the close of the twelfth century. To judge from the handling of the periodization problem, his final acceptance depended in part on a diminished awareness of the fundamental issues raised by the *Historia*. As William of Newburgh pointed out, Geoffrey contradicted Bede on the crucial matter of British dominion south of the Humber. A writer only had to compare the *Historia* with earlier English authorities to see the problems, but William's contemporaries did not use the available data as a control. Over the years the popularity and familiarity of the Galfridian construct seem to have eroded the sense of underlying conflict. Gervase of Canterbury and Roger of Wendover had not witnessed the sudden recovery of the pre-Saxon past, and could hardly be expected to appreciate that Geoffrey's *Historia* represented a radical reassessment of British potential. By the end of the century the Galfridian version of events had contributed so much to the image of Britain's past that the account was not generally seen as an overt challenge to prevailing views. The *Historia* had become part of Insular historical tradition to be treated with the same respect accorded Anglo-Saxon materials. The question of Geoffrey's reliability was not resolved, it was simply forgotten.

4· from the first variant to Layamon

Concern with the contours of Geoffrey's depiction was not the exclusive province of compilers of historical surveys. Redactors and translators of the *Historia* also had to treat the Galfridian framework, but the nature of such undertakings might have been thought to obviate the necessity for confronting the various historical issues raised by the text. Henry of Huntingdon, Robert of Torigni, and Ralph Diceto found it possible to report the contents of the work separately without addressing themselves to the problematic aspects of the Galfridian depiction. The *Epistola ad Warinum* was even included by Henry and Robert in their respective histories, but outside the account proper. If the A-manuscript of Ralph Diceto's historical works does in fact represent the author's own copy, then the presence of the *Historia*-abstract in the collection may be taken as evidence of a similar approach. To their way of thinking, the difficulties arose only when the Galfridian version of events had to be correlated with the testimony of standard authorities. Considered by itself, the implications of the *Historia regum Britanniae* could be ignored, and the deeds of Geoffrey's Britons savoured. Redactors and translators, however, seem unable to draw such a rigorous distinction. In certain cases the handling of the passage of dominion makes clear that they perceived their role as entailing the resolution of major historical problems. Dealing with these issues in the context of Geoffrey's account actually posed some difficulties with which history-writers had not had to contend.

The First Variant is the only version of the *Historia regum Britanniae* to diverge from the Vulgate on the question of periodization. Wace based the *Roman de Brut* on this recension, and his positioning of the dividing line was modelled after his principal source. Layamon produced the only other vernacular paraphrase of the entire *Historia* during the period under discussion, and his

Brut derived from Wace. Because these three texts are interconnected, the redaction and translation activity can be treated as a single complex.

Soon after the publication of Hammer's edition of the First Variant in 1951, Robert A. Caldwell drew attention to the importance of this version for Wace's *Brut*.[1] Many of the items previously thought to have been additions made by Wace could be found in the First Variant. Interestingly enough, the *Roman de Brut* also agreed with the Vulgate against the First Variant on a variety of points. At issue were supplemental data unevenly distributed in Wace's account. The Vulgate became a significant factor in the depiction only after Merlin's prophecy on Vortigern's death, that is upon Aurelius Ambrosius' return from Brittany (HRB, c 119, p 203; FV, 8.1, p 135). Caldwell concluded that Wace had based his vernacular rendering of the *Historia* principally on the First Variant, but had also used a manuscript of the Vulgate for events from the restoration of the Constantinian dynasty onwards.

A decade later Pierre Gallais advanced a radically different view of the interrelationship between the *Roman de Brut* and the First Variant.[2] He objected to the impression conveyed by Caldwell of the manner in which Wace worked: 'Wace n'est-il donc qu'un compilateur? Son œuvre n'est-elle qu'une mosaïque de fragments empruntés aux deux textes, entre lesquels il est perpétuellement en balance?' (Gallais, p 4). Wace would not have followed two manuscripts of the same text. Had he known both versions, Wace could be expected to give precedence to the authentic and much more popular Vulgate. Indeed, Gallais found it unreasonable to suppose that the First Variant circulated prior to 1155 (the completion date of Wace's *Roman de Brut*). No one would have undertaken such extensive revisions in the *Historia* so soon after the work's appearance. The First Variant represented the kind of redaction which was more likely to be found a half-century or even a century later (Gallais, pp 7–9). Gallais restricted his investigation to the Arthurian segment and concluded that a later writer had combined Wace with the Vulgate to produce the First Variant.

There are obvious methodological problems raised by Gallais' concentration on a single section of the three texts. King Arthur's reign forms an undeniable high point, rich in the kind of detail which lends itself to close analysis. But the attention lavished on this monarch bespeaks his very special place among Britain's rulers. To generalize from the handling of Arthuriana is perilous at best, and in fact this section alone admits of Gallais' interpretation. Nevertheless, he poses questions regarding Wace and the First Variant which are central to an understanding of what lies behind certain distinctive features of the accounts.

Gallais' strenuous objection to viewing Wace as a writer who worked from more than one source is difficult to fathom. Caldwell certainly does not imply that the *Roman de Brut* was merely a patchwork of borrowings; indeed, the evidence adduced in support of his argument consists largely of details which could be shown to have come from the First Variant. It is difficult to see how Caldwell's thesis threatened to abase Wace's poetic achievement in the slightest. Gallais clearly places the *Brut* much closer to twelfth-century romance than to twelfth-century historiography, but even the most celebrated narrative poets of the day drew on multiple sources. Where certain popular materials were concerned, such as the Tristan story, romancers undoubtedly selected from among several versions, often combining attractive elements found in different traditions. It would have been surprising had Wace not been something of a *compilateur*. The conscious nature of such decisions only makes the final choices more interesting as potential keys to authorial intent.

Pierre Gallais was wrong in thinking that the First Variant represented a kind of recension unthinkable during Geoffrey's lifetime. The evidence of the compendious surveys suggests just the opposite. Writers who stood in close chronological proximity to the appearance of the *Historia* exhibit a much greater willingness to make far-reaching changes than those a half-century later. Reverence for the Galfridian construct, as preserved in the Vulgate, actually increased with the passing of time. The problematic post-Arthurian segment was omitted by Geffrei Gaimar and Alfred of Beverley but included by Gervase of Canterbury and Roger of Wendover. To judge from the observable trends among twelfth-century historiographers, substantive revisions in the *Historia* would have been more likely, not less, prior to 1155. The anonymous redactor of the First Variant in fact shares many of the same historical concerns which motivated Geffrei Gaimar and Alfred of Beverley.

Neither Caldwell nor Gallais examined the handling of the passage of dominion. Yet several distinctive features of the post-Arthurian segment of the First Variant bear directly on the periodization problem. Wace takes the same characteristic elements as a point of departure for his own depiction. The *Roman de Brut* presupposes a source similar in outline to the First Variant, and an analysis of the periodization in the two works leaves no doubt that Caldwell's view of the interdependent relationship is correct. The divergences from the Vulgate shed considerable light on what motivated the redactor and also on what prompted Wace to give precedence to this version.

The First Variant identifies Gormund's Donation as marking the passage of dominion. The crucial nature of this juncture is signalled by the renaming of the island. The Vulgate makes no mention of such a change in appellation, but Geffrei Gaimar and Alfred of Beverley attest to the speed with which this indicator came to be used in conjunction with Galfridian materials (EDE, lines 19–32, pp 1–2; AB, p 78). At that point in their respective accounts, however, both writers are effecting a transition to English sources and no longer adhere to the *Historia*. One feature of Geoffrey's depiction in fact poses an obstacle to the introduction of the name change, and the redactor of the First Variant can be seen attempting to resolve the difficulty.

The renaming of the island presupposes that the Angles have gained pre-eminence, but the Vulgate consistently terms the Germanic invaders *Saxones* down through Keredic's reign. The First Variant follows Geoffrey in this usage. Gormund explicitly hands Loegria over to the Saxons (HRB, c 186, p 282; FV, 11.7, p 254); yet it is in consequence of this act that the Angles will give their name to the island. The renaming of Britain imputes a dominant role in Insular affairs to a people who have not been previously mentioned. The First Variant circumvents the problem with a simple expedient:

Hinc Saxones Angli vocati sunt qui Loegriam possederunt et ab eis Anglia terra postmodum dicta est. Britonibus enim fugatis atque dispersis, amisit terra nomen Britanniae sicque Angli in ea super reliquias Britonum regnare coeperunt et Britones regni diadema amiserunt nec postea pristinam dignitatem nisi post longum tempus recuperare potuerunt. (FV, 11.7, p 254)

Why the Saxons were henceforth called *Angli* is not explained. The redactor can be shown to have drawn on Bede's *Historia ecclesiastica* earlier, and presumably he knew the famous account of the invasions by the Angles, the Saxons, and the Jutes.[3]

Following Gormund's Donation, the Vulgate describes the parallel systems of tripartite government instituted by both the Britons and the Anglo-Saxons (HRB, c 187, p 283). Consistent with the notion that dominion has already passed to the English, the redactor of the First Variant implies no such equivalence between the two peoples. Driven into Cornwall and Wales, the Britons hide in the mountains and in caves. They harass the Anglo-Saxons and are able to stave off final subjugation for a long time (FV, 11.7, p 254). The First Variant then contrasts the situation in the Celtic domain with that in the heartlands: 'Creati sunt interea plurimi reges Anglorum Saxonum, qui in diversis partibus Loegriae regnaverunt' (FV, 11.8, p 254). The redactor clearly associates political fragmentation with the advent of Anglo-Saxon rule but makes no mention of any attendant disorder. Instead of balancing the methods of government, he juxtaposes the barbarism of the Britons and the apparent stability of the English kingdoms. Æthelberht is said to have been one of the English rulers, and mention of his name provides a transition to Augustine's mission.

In marked contrast to the British bias of the Vulgate Version, the First Variant treats the conversion from a decidedly English perspective. Geoffrey of Monmouth derived his basic information on Augustine's missionary activity from Bede, but, as happens so frequently in the *Historia*, the material was manipulated for his own purposes. The redactor of the First Variant makes extensive changes in this section, bringing the account into agreement with Anglo-Saxon tradition. A new orientation is clear from the outset. In the Vulgate Gregory the Great sends Augustine *in Britanniam* (HRB, c 188, p 283), but the First Variant reads *in Angliam* (FV, 11.8, p 254). The alteration reflects the island's renaming described in the preceding chapter. The redactor, however, does not carry through with the new appellation and follows the Vulgate hereafter.

Geoffrey of Monmouth devotes no space to actually depicting Augustine's saving work among the Anglo-Saxons. Pope Gregory charges Augustine with the conversion of the pagan English, and then the Vulgate moves immediately to the current situation in the British domain: 'In parte autem Britonum adhuc vigebat christianitas, quae, a tempore Eleutherii papae habita, nunquam inter eos defecerat' (HRB, c 188, p 283). The British Church has a strong prior claim (cf HRB, cc 72–3, pp 144–5) and has maintained the faith, though sorely tested by Gormund. At the time of Augustine's arrival it is clearly not the Britons who need spiritual guidance.

The structure of this section of the Vulgate determines how Augustine's subsequent activities are viewed. Although charged only with converting the Anglo-Saxons, he seems to interject himself immediately into the system of ecclesiastical administration evolved by the British Church. Geoffrey eliminates the doctrinal issues, and offers essentially an undifferentiated view of Western Christendom at the end of the sixth century. By not describing Augustine's missionary work, the portrait becomes extremely unflattering. The reference to the long history and current well-being of the British Church serves to make Augustine's interference obviously unwarranted. The slaughter at Chester becomes the awful consequence of a jurisdictional dispute initiated by a meddlesome prelate (HRB, cc 188–9, pp 283–5).

In the First Variant much more emphasis is placed on Augustine's winning of proselytes. Æthelberht's importance to the initial stage of the conversion effort is described, together with his baptism and the general success of the mission:

Veniens itaque Augustinus in Cantiam susceptus est a rege Athelbricto gratanter et, eo permittente et concedente, verbum Dei genti praedicavit Anglorum et signo fidei eos insignivit. Deinde, non multo post Athelbrictus rex ipse cum ceteris baptismatis sacramentum consecutus est. Suscepta igitur in Cantia ab Anglis Christianitate, diffusa est per totam Loegriam fides Iesu Christi usque ad fines Britonum. (FV, 11.8, p 254)

The nature of Augustine's achievement can now be seen, and it is against this backdrop that the redactor places the encounter with the British churchmen. Moreover, he suppresses the comment on Pope Eleutherius and the state of the faith among the Britons. The Galfridian version has been recast in a decidedly Anglo-Saxon mould.

This identifiable shift in the focus of the First Variant is only temporary. The redactor corrects the portrait of Augustine and then follows the outlines of the Vulgate closely down to Cadwaladr's day. The account of Cadwallon's turbulent reign has been greatly compressed, but it is not possible to see the changes as part of a thoroughgoing reorientation. Bede's portrayal of Cadwallon is extremely harsh (HE, 2.20, pp 202–4; 3.1, pp 212–14), but the First Variant shows no trace of influence from this quarter (FV, 11.9–14, pp 256–61). Although the redactor knew and used the *Historia ecclesiastica*, there is nothing to suggest that he selected materials from the Vulgate on Cadwallon with Bede's characterization in mind. Not even the material on Augustine's missionary activity can be shown to have come directly from Bede. Quite clearly, no parallel historiographic depiction was used to provide a consistent check on Geoffrey of Monmouth.

Cadwaladr's reign witnesses a series of catastrophes which result in large-scale Saxon invasions of a virtually uninhabited island. At this juncture the Vulgate contains a second comment on the loss of British sovereignty: 'Ab illo tempore potestas Britonum in insula cessavit et Angli regnare coeperunt' (HRB, c 204, p 301). The First Variant contains an expanded statement:

Ab illo autem tempore potestas Britonum cessavit et Angli in totum regnum regnare coeperunt, Adestano rege facto, qui primus inter eos diadema portavit. Pacem et concordiam tamquam fratres inter se habentes, agros coluerunt, civitates et oppida reaedificaverunt et magistratus et potestates in urbibus constituentes, leges, quas de terra sua adduxerant, subiectis populis tradiderunt servandas, ducatus et honores, prout Britones ante habuerant, inter se dividentes, summa pace et tranquillitate terram desiderabilem incoluerunt. (FV, 11.16, p 263)

The redactor has moved up the information on Athelstan and the Anglo-Saxons' prudent behaviour found at the very end of the Vulgate (cf HRB, c 207, p 303). In the process, however, Athelstan and Cadwaladr have become contemporaries.

The anonymous redactor has attempted to reconcile two statements which occur in the Vulgate at different points. He appears to reason that, if the Anglo-Saxons overran the heartlands and 'began to rule,' then Athelstan, identified as the first true English king, must have gained power in Cadwaladr's day. Geoffrey, of course, used the two comments to make clear that the English had not gained pre-eminence in Insular affairs merely by conquering a deserted island. The institution of strong centralized government under Athelstan marked their assumption of a leading role, because in Geoffrey's view unified rule was a prerequisite for significant achievement. The First Variant bears witness to the strength of the traditional association of territorial control with historical pre-eminence, irrespective of the style of government involved. The redactor missed the entire point of the arrangement of materials in the Vulgate and obliterated what Geoffrey regarded as a crucial time-lag. The Galfridian effort to separate the territorial issue from other possible indicators breaks down in a redaction made soon after the *Historia* first appeared.

The handling of Athelstan in the First Variant seriously distorts the chronology. Cadwaladr's death is placed in the year 689 (FV, 11.17, p 264), and by making the two rulers contemporaries, the redactor betrays considerable uncertainty regarding Athelstan's identity. He either failed to recognize the tenth-century monarch or assumed the existence of two like-named sovereigns.[4] The Vulgate does not date Athelstan's accession, and the account moves very quickly at the end. Geoffrey no longer proceeds systematically, but rather makes sizable chronological leaps. Under the circumstances some degree of confusion is perhaps understandable.

Because the redactor has already used the material on Athelstan and the rebuilding of the island, these matters are not repeated at the end. The First Variant reports the Britons' change of name and then adds the following comment: 'Sed illi Britones qui in parte boreali Angliae remanserunt, a lingua Britannica degenerati, numquam Loegriam vel ceteras australes partes recuperaverunt' (FV, 11.17, p 264).[5] The text concludes with a shortened version of the epilogue in which the reader is not referred to any specific historians for information on subsequent events (FV, 11.18, p 264).

In the conflate manuscripts of the First Variant the Vulgate periodization is restored. Gormund's Donation no longer marks the passage of dominion, and the parallel systems of tripartite government among the Britons and the Anglo-Saxons are once again described (FV, 11.7, p 192). The English perspective on Augustine's mission found in the First Variant has also been replaced by the pro-British version in the Vulgate (FV, 11.8, pp 192–3). Those distinctive features of the First Variant, which bespeak the intrusion of an Anglo-Saxon viewpoint, have been eliminated in favour of the Vulgate depiction.

The c-text does, however, retain the handling of Athelstan (FV, 11.16, p

206). Despite marked preference for the Vulgate, this redactor seems to have found the passage in the First Variant an appealing solution to an otherwise perplexing problem. But because he essentially follows the Vulgate for the post-Arthurian era, the reference to Athelstan and the progress of the reconstruction are repeated at the end, where the materials were originally found. The c-redactor is aware of the duplication and notes 'ut praedictum est' (FV, 11.17, p 208).[6]

The manuscript transmission of the First Variant is extremely interesting in light of the trends observed among historiographers in the twelfth century. The evidence would seem to indicate an analogous drift away from the importance of prior English tradition and toward greater reverence for the Galfridian construct as preserved in the Vulgate. Before this argument can be pursued, it will be necessary to establish beyond any reasonable doubt that Wace drew on the First Variant prior to 1155. He too added material from the Vulgate, and in fact began to use this version at approximately the same point selected by redactors of the conflate manuscripts.[7] On the question of periodization, however, Wace can be shown to have followed the First Variant, elaborating key points and even correcting the confusion over Athelstan. The interrelationship between the two texts affords additional insight into the concerns of writers active during Geoffrey's lifetime.

With the popularity of the *Historia* came the desirability of rendering the account into the vernacular. The thought seems to have occurred independently to more than one writer beginning around the middle of the century. Wace's *Roman de Brut* may be the most famous example, but it is not alone. Fragments of several efforts in this direction are extant. Wace dates the completion of his metrical paraphrase in 1155 (RdB, lines 14,863–6, p 779). The *Munich Brut* appears to be slightly earlier, but the dating of the various fragmentary versions poses major difficulties.[8] The question of priority cannot be resolved satisfactorily on the basis of current manuscript evidence.

Fortunately, these dating problems have no bearing on the present discussion. There is nothing to suggest the interdependence of the surviving attempts, and none of the remnants includes the post-Arthurian epoch. Although portions of various texts may have been lost, it is not reasonable to assume that each fragment represents part of a completed translation. Wace's *Brut* remains the earliest version of the entire *Historia*. In terms of influence on subsequent generations of writers, Wace also stands alone. The *Roman de Brut* belongs at the head of the tradition of chronicle-writing bearing the name of Britain's eponym.

Wace's handling of the periodization problem is modelled after the First Variant. In the *Roman de Brut* the British loss of territorial control during the reign of Keredic/Cariz marks the passage of dominion. Wace notes the accession of this monarch, and then previews the events which would bring about the renaming of the island:

> Cariz fud puis reis de la terre,
> Mes tute la perdi par guerre;
> Dolenz fud e maleürus
> E a tute gent haïnus.
> En sun tens vint la grant surverse
> De paens e de gent adverse
> Que Gurmunt amena par mer,
> Bien en avez oï parler,
> Ki firent la destructiun
> Dunt Bretaine perdi sun nun.
> (RDB, lines 13,375–84, pp 698–9)

Unlike the First Variant, Wace introduces the name change before recounting the actual occurrences. The passage cited above provides necessary historical perspective and signals the importance of what is to follow.

One interesting divergence from both the Vulgate and the First Variant would appear to be closely connected with this preview of the passage of dominion. Whereas the *Historia* has Gormund cross with his African hordes *ad/in Britanniam* (HRB, c 184, p 281; FV, 11.6, p 253), Wace anticipates the outcome and speaks of the ruler's desire to invade *Engleterre* (RDB, line 13,420, p 700). After Brutus renames Albion, the island is always called *Bretaine* down to this point in the account. Following initial mention of the second name change, however, the usage shifts abruptly. The new appellation is employed regularly, though not exclusively down to the end.[9] In the First Variant Augustine is sent by Pope Gregory *in Angliam* (FV, 11.8, p 254) but the redactor continues to use *Britannia* hereafter, even though the island has already been renamed. Whether the single example in the First Variant inspired Wace to use *Engleterre* with greater consistency is difficult to say.

Wace returns to the subject of the change of name as he recounts the aftermath of Cariz' reign. It is at this juncture that the First Variant describes the renaming of Britain (FV, 11.7, p 254). In the *Roman de Brut* Gormund explicitly hands the island over to the Saxons (RDB, lines 13,634–40, p 713), leaving again the problem of accounting for the derivation of the new name:

> Cil unt la terre recuillie,
> Ki mult l'aveient encovie.
> Pur un lignage dunt cil furent

Ki la terre primes reçurent
Se firent Engleis apeler
Pur lur orine remenbrer,
E Englelande unt apelee
La terre ki lur ert dunee.
Tant dit Engleterre en franceis
Cum dit Englelande en engleis;
Terre a Engleis, ço dit li nuns,
Ço en est l'espositiuns.
(RDB, lines 13,641–52, pp 713–14)

Wace is obviously following the First Variant and has attempted to provide a more satisfactory explanation than that found in his source: 'Hinc Saxones Angli vocati sunt qui Loegriam possederunt et ab eis Anglia terra postmodum dicta est' (FV, 11.7, p 254). Although there is nothing to suggest Wace's use of the *Historia ecclesiastica*, Bede states that the Angles' Continental homeland was called *Angulus* (HE, 1.15, p 50). This popular tradition probably lies behind Wace's view that the island's new overlords called themselves *Engleis*, 'Pur lur orine remenbrer' (RDB, line 13,646, p 714).

The name change heralds the advent of Anglo-Saxon dominion, and Wace recalls the long period during which the isle was known as Britain (RDB, lines 13, 653–8, p 714). The new rulers are not content with a single sign of their ascendancy and rename unspecified cities as well (RDB, lines 13,659–62, pp 714–15). The island begins to take on a distinctly English appearance in consequence of Gormund's Donation. The toponymic importance of this event further underscores the inescapable fact that dominion has passed from the hands of the Britons. The First Variant mentions only the renaming of the island itself.

Wace can be seen elaborating and clarifying the periodization in the First Variant, a trend which continues as the fragmentation of early Anglo-Saxon rule comes under discussion (RDB, lines 13,663–82, pp 715–16). The *Roman de Brut* provides information on the English mode of governance at the same juncture as its principal source (FV, 11.8, p 254). Like the redactor of the First Variant, Wace eliminates the Britons from consideration, but he provides a more detailed account of the difficulties which the Anglo-Saxons encountered in selecting a king. Unable to agree upon a single ruler, the English decide to partition their lands:

Engleis voldrent rei establir,
Mes ne se porent assentir
Que un rei sulement eüssent

E a un rei tuit suget fussent.
Ne s'acorderent mie a un,
Ainz firent, par cunseil commun,
Plusurs reis en plusurs cuntrees
Si unt les terres devisees.
Plusurs feiz s'entreguerrierent
E plusurs feiz se rapaierent.
Si cum chascun plus fort esteit
Sur le plus fieble cunquereit.
(RdB, lines 13,663–74, p 715)

The First Variant provides only a general statement which leaves much unexplained: 'Creati sunt interea plurimi reges Anglorum Saxonum, qui in diversis partibus Loegriae regnaverunt' (FV, 11,8, p 254). Wace 1/ makes clear the reason for the divisions, 2/ affords a glimpse of the decision-making process, and 3/ describes the resultant turmoil. The English are said to have lived without the rule of law and without the faith until the coming of Augustine (RdB, lines 13,675–82, p 716).

The First Variant offered an English view of the conversion (FV, 11.8, pp 254–5), and Wace moves further in this direction. The arrival in Canterbury, the baptism of Æthelberht, and the general success of the mission are all described as in the First Variant (RdB, lines 13,683–710, pp 716–17). Like his source, Wace makes no mention of Pope Eleutherius or the situation in the British domain. A lengthy account is now added on how Augustine carried out his saving work in the face of hardship and personal abuse (RdB, lines 13,711–812, pp 717–23). Wace seems to have drawn on a life of the saint, but the account does not derive from any version discovered to date.[10] Whereas Geoffrey of Monmouth found Bede's portrait of a tactless, hard-bitten missionary ideal for his purposes, Wace replaces the image with that of the long-suffering prelate of English hagiographical tradition. The encounter with British churchmen and the slaughter at Chester are then recounted without major revision (RdB, lines 13,813–926, pp 723–8).

Wace found the portrait of Augustine in need of further change, but, like the redactor of the First Variant, he did not use a parallel historiographic depiction as a continuous check on the *Historia*. The *Roman de Brut* contains nothing to indicate direct dependence on any of the standard English authorities, even though Wace appears to have used William of Malmesbury's *Gesta regum Anglorum* a short time later in the *Roman de Rou*.[11]

For anyone who adhered to the Galfridian framework, some mention of Athelstan's significance was well-nigh unavoidable. Wace faced the added complication of having two divergent and equally unsatisfactory views in front of him. He drew on both the Vulgate and the First Variant in the latter portions of the account, and each of these versions posed a special problem where Athelstan was concerned. In the Vulgate Geoffrey's contention that Anglo-Saxon pre-eminence must be dated from the institution of unified rule in the tenth century was not consonant with Wace's own views on the passage of dominion. The First Variant only compounded the difficulties by making Cadwaladr and Athelstan contemporaries. Unlike the anonymous redactor, Wace knew full well the identity of the English king in question. Neither the Galfridian periodization nor the confusion surrounding Athelstan's dates were allowed to stand. To deal satisfactorily with both problems, Wace found it necessary to define Athelstan's importance to Insular history in considerable detail.

The *Roman de Brut* contains not one, but two passages on Athelstan. The first occurs following the slaughter at Chester and is without parallel in either the Vulgate or the First Variant. When the Britons attempt to avenge the massacre, the *Historia* draws special attention to three leaders: Blederic, duke of Cornwall; Margadud, king of the Demetae; and Cadfan, king of the Venedoti (HRB, c 189, p 285; FV, 11.8, pp 255–6). According to Wace, the Britons made substantial territorial gains under these three leaders and maintained effective control of the lands for a long time. It was Athelstan who finally conquered the territory and drove the Britons beyond the River Wye (RdB, lines 13,929–46, p 729).

Wace jumps from the first decade of the seventh century down to the second quarter of the tenth previewing subsequent realignments. The passage is inserted for the purpose of defining Athelstan's importance and providing some perspective on the British achievement in question. Wace assesses this king's reign strictly in terms of the expansion of the Anglo-Saxon domain, and no mention is made of the institution of centralized government. For Wace territorial control is the sole criterion for determining the balance of power between the contending peoples. Just as dominion passed from the Britons in the wake of Gormund's conquest of the island, so now Athelstan's contribution to Anglo-Saxon history must be assessed in territorial terms.

From this point down to Cadwaladr's reign the *Roman de Brut* offers a close paraphrase of the *Historia*.[12] Following the plague and mass emigrations by the Britons, Germanic settlers arrive in large numbers and assume undisputed control of the island's heartlands (RdB, lines 14,719–30, pp 771–2). The territorial balance shifts for the last time as the Saxons prosper and multiply. The settlers bring to the new land their ancestral customs and laws, thereby preserving continuity with the past (RdB, lines 14,731–8, p 772).[13] Wace returns to the toponymic importance of Anglo-Saxon dominion, a subject broached earlier. The process is described in much greater detail, and some of the more obvious changes are enumerated (RdB, lines 14,739–50, pp 772–3; cf lines 13,659–62, pp 714–15).

What began after Gormund's Donation receives fresh impetus from the tremendous influx of settlers. Such new arrivals could be expected to have a stronger sense of their Germanic heritage than Anglo-Saxons whose forefathers had immigrated perhaps as much as two centuries earlier. Even so, the process described by Wace is a lengthy one. The areas in which the older British usage prevails are gradually reduced until only Wales remains (RdB, lines 14,751–6, p 773). In the *Roman de Brut* the geographic distribution of personal and place names mirrors the progress of Anglo-Saxon culture.

The endpoint in the development is of considerable importance. The moment when Anglo-Saxon culture reached its full extent brings a demarcation which would remain both an identifying feature of England's geography and a significant political factor. Because the juncture is so crucial, Wace identifies the king whose reign witnessed effective completion of the process:

A cel tens ert Adelstan reis;
Ço fud li premiers des Engleis
Ki ot tute Engleterre en baille
Fors sul Guales e Cornuaille;
Premier fud enoinz e sacrez
E premierement curunez.
(RdB, lines 14,757–62, pp 773–4)

The completion of the cultural expansion coincided with the rule of Athelstan under whom the territorial limits of Anglo-Saxon dominion were established. To Wace's way of thinking, the culture spread in the wake of military conquest and occupation.

Wace combines the notion of a close correlation between territorial and cultural expansion with Geoffrey's statement on Athelstan as the first true Anglo-Saxon king. This passage does not constitute a break with the earlier definition of Athelstan's historical importance. Wace merely elaborates the consequences of a greatly enlarged Anglo-Saxon domain. Territorial control comes first, with the cultural and toponymic changes following. The sacring of Athelstan becomes an acknowledgment that he, by dint of military prowess, had a major role in giving shape to Anglo-Saxon England.

Wace's view of Athelstan's importance differs markedly from that found in the *Historia*. There is no sense that the reign of this tenth-century sovereign brought a radical departure in the Anglo-Saxon style of government. Although Wace notes the fragmentation of early English rule, he stresses a basic cultural unity which cut across the political boundaries within the Anglo-Saxon domain. Different groups may have arrived at widely separated times, but the settlers shared their Continental Germanic origins. Wace sees an underlying homogeneity of language and culture writ large in England's toponymy. Political divisions existed among the Anglo-Saxons, but on a map of the island it was not this fragmentation which distinguished their domain from the lands under Celtic control. The demarcation was cultural, not institutional.

The *Roman de Brut* depicts the process by which one Insular culture eventually yielded to another. Territorial control is the prime requisite for achieving pre-eminence. Athelstan pushes back the Britons, and his conquests bring the establishment of Anglo-Saxon culture in areas where Celtic usage formerly held sway. Unlike Geoffrey of Monmouth, Wace correlates military and cultural domination. Geoffrey consistently downplays the consequences of territorial control in order to make his didactic point regarding unified rule. Wace sees the developments rather differently, and there can be little doubt that his view was the more conventional of the two.

Following the reference to Athelstan's sacring, Wace provides supplemental data on the ruler's lineage (RdB, lines 14,763–74, p 774). Some degree of genealogical precision is appropriate for so important a figure, but the additional information seems to have a further narrative function. According to Wace, many allege that Athelstan was the bastard son of Edward the Elder. Edward undertook a journey to Rome in order to pay the Peter's Pence. One of Athelstan's illustrious ancestors was in fact Ine who initiated the practice. This is the same Ine who ruled over Wessex after Cadwaladr's abdication (cf HE, 5.7, p 472; ASC, p 24; HA, 2.6, p 108). Having digressed from the *Historia* in order to preview the expansion of Anglo-Saxon culture, the mention of Ine brings the discussion back to the late seventh century. Wace picks up the chronological thread with Cadwaladr's exile.

Wace's second comment on Athelstan occurs at that point in the account where the First Variant describes the English ruler as Cadwaladr's contemporary. The genealogical information supplied in the *Roman de Brut* establishes the chronological interrelationship between the two figures and corrects the confusion in the First Variant. Here as elsewhere, Wace can be seen reacting to the characteristic features of this version of the *Historia*.

Although Wace had no choice but to deal with Athelstan at length, the outlines of the English expansion provide a larger context within which the Galfridian version of events must be seen. Gormund's Donation marked the effective end of British rule, but centuries would be required for the Anglo-

Saxons to achieve full territorial and cultural ascendancy. The early kingdoms do not serve as the principal identifying feature of a new era. In Wace's view the common Germanic heritage of the invaders transcended their political fragmentation and set them off from the indigenous Celts. Consequently, the spread of Anglo-Saxon culture takes on crucial significance. Wace does not analyse each event recounted from the *Historia* in terms of this process, nor are the various stages in the development specified. Under Athelstan, however, Anglo-Saxon culture is said to have reached its fullest geographical extent, thereby accounting for the significance attached to this ruler by Geoffrey. Wace redefines Athelstan's importance, and by so doing justifies the Galfridian depiction. The Anglo-Saxon viewpoint now tolerates Geoffrey's Britons, because the overall shape of developments is clear.

At the conclusion of the *Roman de Brut* the campaign of guerrilla warfare conducted by Yvor and Yni is described. There then follows the Britons' name change, together with the possible etymologies of the term 'Welsh' (RdB, lines 14,843–58, p 778; FV, 11.17, p 264; cf HRB, c 207, pp 302–3). Geoffrey's epilogue has left no trace in Wace's own final comments.

The handling of the periodization problem in the *Roman de Brut* leaves no doubt but that Wace relied heavily on the First Variant. Several features of his account can only be explained as responses to items peculiar to this version of the *Historia*. Although the conflate manuscripts of the First Variant exhibit some similarities with Wace in the use of the Vulgate, they lack the distinctive treatment of the passage of dominion. That more than one writer should have decided independently to supplement the account of the reigns of Aurelius Ambrosius, Utherpendragon, and Arthur is hardly surprising. The periodization, however, marks the First Variant and Wace as products of the initial phase in Geoffrey's reception. Underlying the two depictions of the post-Arthurian era is the same desire to reconcile the Galfridian construct with English tradition found in Geffrei Gaimar and Alfred of Beverley. Wace goes to considerable lengths to elaborate the version of events in the First Variant, and by so doing he makes clear why this redaction was given precedence over the Vulgate. He too perceived a need to reach some form of accommodation with the familiar contours of Anglo-Saxon history.

Wace attests to the availability of the First Variant prior to 1155. The speed with which this redaction appeared becomes less startling when viewed against the backdrop of Geffrei Gaimar's and Alfred of Beverley's similar concerns. The conflate manuscripts of the First Variant with their restoration of the Vulgate periodization were produced at a later date. Here again the handling of the Galfridian construct parallels trends observed in the historical surveys. I am inclined to see in the conflation of the First Variant with the Vulgate the same diminished sense of the fundamental historical issues. At some point, probably toward the close of the twelfth century, what motivated both the anonymous redactor and Wace gave way to reverence for the authentic Vulgate Version. Just as writers once found it impossible to deal with the *Historia* without attempting some reconciliation with Anglo-Saxon tradition, so now the First Variant could not be copied without correcting at least the major divergences. I am speaking here only of texts produced by English and Anglo-Norman writers. That an Irishman or a Welshman might have very different reasons for preferring the Vulgate is obvious.

Another complete *Brut* is not found until Layamon provides the first English language paraphrase of Wace around the turn of the century. Although derivative of the *Roman de Brut*, Layamon's text diverges from its principal source on several key points and, in fact, represents something of a step backwards where the periodization of Insular history is concerned. The alterations made by Layamon bespeak nothing so much as the fact that the entire question has ceased to be a matter of major concern.

Layamon follows Wace in designating Gormund's Donation as the effective end of British rule. The renaming of the island, the more general toponymic importance of the take-over, and the characterization of early Anglo-Saxon rule are all borrowed (LB, lines 14,668–94, pp 767–8). The section retains Wace's ordering of the constituent elements, but certain items receive elaboration.

Perhaps the most interesting example of how Layamon extrapolates from the *Roman de Brut* involves the fragmentation of early English rule. Wace's account implies that a meeting was convoked by the Anglo-Saxons to select a king (RdB, lines 13,663–70, p 715). Layamon converts this somewhat indistinct gathering into a great assembly at London (LB, lines 14,684–5, p 768). When agreement cannot be reached, five kings are set over the Anglo-Saxons (LB, lines 14,686–8, p 768). Wace merely states that the English established 'Plusurs reis en plusurs cuntrees' (RdB, line 13,669, p 715).[14] Although the number of kingdoms varies considerably in the twelfth century, I know of no other writer who fixes the number at five.[15] The outcome, of course, is the same. A period of civil strife ensues, which comes to an end with Augustine's arrival.[16]

Layamon encounters real difficulties with Wace's first reference to Athelstan. Following the slaughter at Chester, the discussion turns to the British leaders Blederic, Cadfan, and Margadud. Thanks to the efforts of these three, the Britons maintain control of considerable territory until Athelstan drives them from the heartlands for the last time (LB, lines 14,930–3, p 782; RdB, lines 13,929–46, p 729). Layamon then describes how Athelstan marched against Margadud and forced the South Welsh to retreat beyond the River Wye (LB, lines 14,938–44, p 782).

The slaughter at Chester is thought to have occurred between 613 and 616. That Athelstan could have waged war against Margadud, who lived at the time of the infamous massacre, is clearly an impossibility. Layamon has misunderstood Wace's comments on Athelstan, and the source of the confusion is, I think, clear. In the *Roman de Brut* Wace specifies the lands seized by the three British leaders, and then states: 'Ço tindrent Bretun lungement; / Mes Adelstan quant il regna / Ultre Tambre les esluina' (RdB, lines 13,938–40, p 729). Layamon has taken the pronoun as referring to Blederic, Cadfan, and Margadud, whereas Wace clearly meant the Britons. The fact that these events took place *quant il regna* makes Athelstan and the three British leaders contemporaries. The lines 'Mais Aedelstan tant les destreinst / Que ultre Waie les enpeinst' (RdB, lines 13,945–6, p 729) were interpreted by Layamon in the same way.

Following the plague in Cadwaladr's lifetime, Continental Saxons land in droves (LB, lines 15,922–40, p 830). With these settlers comes Athelstan, who is subsequently crowned king at London (LB, lines 15,941–2, p 830). Layamon then follows Wace in adding the information on Athelstan's lineage and Peter's Pence (LB, lines 15,943–64, pp 830–2; RdB, lines 14,763–74, p 774). No mention is made of Athelstan's being the first king to rule over all England. Wace's description of the spread of Anglo-Saxon culture in the wake of the landings now follows, rather than precedes, the background material on Athelstan. In the *Roman de Brut* the reign of the tenth-century sovereign marks the point in Insular history when English customs and English usage expanded to their fullest territorial extent (RdB, lines 14,715–62, p 771–4). Like Wace, Layamon sees the influx of settlers as giving fresh impetus to the spread of Anglo-Saxon culture. Athelstan, however, has become Cadwaladr's contemporary and can no longer mark the endpoint in the development. In striking contrast to the *Roman de Brut*, Athelstan now rules at the start of this period of expansion. The fact that the island begins to take on a decidedly English appearance prompts Cadwaladr to plan the reconquest of his homeland from Athelstan (LB, lines 15,965–92, pp 832–4). The preparations are abandoned after a vision. From this point through to the conclusion Layamon adheres closely to Wace's account.

Wace's effort to reconcile the Galfridian and Anglo-Saxon views on periodization depends upon Athelstan. Layamon introduces a degree of confusion remarkable even in an age which exhibits some uncertainty regarding the identity of this sovereign. The arrangement of materials in the *Roman de Brut* is made to yield two Athelstans. The first seems to result from a misunderstanding of Wace's text, the second from a combination of factors. Layamon may have known a redaction of the *Historia* in which Cadwaladr and Athelstan were treated as contemporaries. In all likelihood, however, Wace also drew on such a recension and included the supplemental information on Athelstan's line to correct this notion. Layamon retains the additional materials, even expands the section, but makes the English king Cadwaladr's rival for dominion over the island. Wace's description of the spread of Anglo-Saxon culture is converted to use as a motivational device, and no longer serves to preview nearly two and a half centuries of English history.

Much more than time and language separates the two metrical paraphrases. Wace is acutely aware of the existence of an alternative viewpoint. He perceives the need to both correlate and adjust Geoffrey's periodization in order to bring about accommodation with Anglo-Saxon tradition. The details are omitted, as indeed they must be, but the sketches of growing English ascendancy serve as a reminder that the concluding sections of Geoffrey's *Historia* must be seen in a larger context. This sense of two parallel chronologies is missing from Layamon's account. He exhibits little concern for the kind of historical considerations which underlie Wace's depiction of the sixth and seventh centuries. In this regard Layamon clearly reflects more general trends around 1200.

Wace and Laymon perceive their tasks very differently. At the close of the century the need to reconcile Geoffrey's periodization with Anglo-Saxon tradition no longer dominates usage patterns. With chronological remove writers seem to lose any appreciation of the challenge which the *Historia* posed to conventional thinking at the time of its appearance. In the interim between the two completed *Bruts*, the Galfridian construct gained acceptance, and Geoffrey himself became an acknowledged authority. Although texts continue to bear the marks of earlier struggles with the passage of dominion, the issue is essentially dead by 1200. Whereas Wace elaborates the periodization in the First Variant with an eye to clarifying the interrelationship between two very different views of sixth- and seventh-century Insular history, Layamon exhibits no similar concerns. He does not give precedence to the Vulgate Version, but nonetheless shares with the redactors who conflated the First Variant a diminished awareness of the fundamental historical issues. The century ends, as it did among historians, with a lost sense of conflict and a lack of understanding for what motivated writers fifty or sixty years earlier.

NOTES

WORKS CITED

INDEX

NOTES

INTRODUCTION

1 For a convenient survey of the events and the evidence see Fisher, *The Anglo-Saxon Age*, 1–16.
2 Use of the designation *litus Saxonicum* for sections of the Channel coast both in Britain and on the Continent is attested only in the *Notitia dignitatum* (probably a fifth-century compilation), ed Seeck, Oc 1.36 (p 104); 5.132 (p 121); 28 (pp 180–1); and 37–8 (pp 204–7). Although this name obviously antedates the *Notitia dignitatum*, at what point it gained currency and its precise meaning have long been debated. I find Stephen Johnson's interpretation of the evidence most persuasive: *The Roman Forts of the Saxon Shore*. Donald A. White's contention that Carausius constructed the system of fortifications to guard against a possible invasion by Diocletian has not found wide acceptance: *Litus Saxonicum: The British Saxon Shore*. See especially Johnson's discussion of the strategic value of the forts against sea-borne raiders: *The Roman Forts of the Saxon Shore*, 114–31. No medieval historian employs the designation 'Saxon Shore' for the coastal area in question here.
3 Gildas connects the stone wall and adjacent *vallum* with two successful British appeals to the Romans for help: DEB, cc 15–18, pp 33–5. See Stevens, 'Gildas Sapiens,' 356–9. The Gildasian chronology is fuzzy, but these attempts to secure Britain against Hiberno-Pictish incursions fall between the execution of Maximus in 388 (DEB, c 13, p 33) and the appeal to Aetius in his third consulship, 446–50 (DEB, c 20, p 36). Bede follows Orosius, and ascribes the original construction of the wall to Severus in the second century: HE, 1.5, p 26; Orosius, HAP, 7.17, p 475. Bede also includes Gildas' attractive account of the British appeals, explicitly stating that this later construction involved the substantial rebuilding of Severus' fortifications: HE, 1.12, pp 40–4. See Miller, 'Bede's Use of Gildas,' 243–6. Gildas also knew Orosius, but probably did not follow him far enough to discover the passage on Severus: Stevens, 'Gildas Sapiens,' 358.
4 The *De excidio* has generally been dated c 540. For a review of the scholarship on this question see O'Sullivan, pp 77–86. After examining all the evidence, O'Sullivan concludes that the years c 515–530 are a somewhat likelier range 'with more probability in the earlier part of that period' (p 178). Given the nature of the difficulties, alternative dates will almost certainly continue to be proposed.
5 See also Fisher's discussion of Gildas and Bede on this point: *The Anglo-Saxon Age*, 16–22.
6 DEB, cc 15–21, pp 33–6. As has frequently been remarked, some combination of actual occurrences with folkloristic patterns may lie behind Gildas' account: Gransden, pp 4–5. See also Bede, HE, 1.12–14, pp 40–8.

7 Eutropius, *Breviarium*, ed Droysen, 9.21, p 162. See Donald Atkinson, '*Classis Britannica*,' 7. There is no evidence that Gildas knew Eutropius.

8 Stevens, 'Gildas Sapiens,' 359–60.

9 Stenton, *Anglo-Saxon England*, 19–23.

10 The relative chronology hinges on the much-debated *quadragesimus quartus annus* passage in Gildas (DEB, c 26, p 40). The obscurity of the text notwithstanding, I am inclined to agree with O'Sullivan (pp 134–57) that Gildas places the battle in relation to the British resurgence under Ambrosius Aurelianus. Bede dates the victory at Mount Badon forty-four years after the arrival of Hengist and Horsa (HE, 1.16, p 54).

11 Bede did, however, regard the Anglo-Saxon *adventus* as a significant turning point in Insular history. The Battle of Mount Badon is only one of five occasions on which he dates events relative to the first landings: HE, 1.16, p 54; 1.23, p 68; 2.14, p 186; 5.23, p 560; and 5.24, p 562.

12 See annals 456, 465, 473, 477, and 491: ASC, pp 10–11.

13 See for example Henry of Huntingdon, HA, 1.4–5, pp 8–10.

14 Cf Fisher, *The Anglo-Saxon Age*, 22–8.

15 Sisam has convincingly argued for the relatively late date of pedigrees which extend the line back beyond Woden: 'Anglo-Saxon Royal Genealogies,' 287–348. See also Dumville, 'The Anglian Collection of Royal Genealogies and Regnal Lists,' 48.

16 Bede simply observes that many Anglo-Saxon royal families traced their line of descent back to Woden. He does not identify this figure: HE, 1.15, p 50. The annalists of the *Anglo-Saxon Chronicle* are equally vague, even though Woden appears in numerous genealogies. That medieval writers had no clear conception of the reason for Woden's importance becomes clear in Æthelweard's chronicle. Æthelweard states that Woden was *rex multitudinis barbarorum* (ÆC, 1.4, p 9). Harrison has argued that Woden may actually be a deified mortal: 'Woden,' 351–6.

17 The best discussion of this point is provided by Dumville, 'Kingship, Genealogies and Regnal Lists,' 72–104.

18 Hanning's perceptive analysis of the *De excidio* focuses on Gildas' intent: *The Vision of History in Early Britain*, 44–62.

19 Subsequently, Gildas does provide information on five corrupt kings, but these data are only incidental to invectives heaped upon their royal persons: DEB, cc 28–33, pp 41–4.

20 HB, cc 57–66, pp 202–9. The compiler used a Northumbrian regnal list as a frame for his meagre information on the Britons, 'almost certainly because there was no comparably coherent structure to be derived from his Brittonic source-materials': Dumville, 'Sub-Roman Britain: History and Legend,' 177. See also the *Annales Cambriae*, ed Phillimore, pp 154–9.

21 *Epitoma chronicon*, ed Mommsen, p 472.

22 Because the *De excidio* divides into an historical survey (cc 2–26) and a much longer homiletic section (cc 27–110), the unity of the text has repeatedly been called into question. O'Sullivan marshals an impressive body of internal evidence to support both the integrity of the *De excidio* and Gildas' authorship of the whole: O'Sullivan, pp 48–76. Yet the Sawley manuscript does provide evidence of the separate transmission of the historical section in the early thirteenth century: Dumville, 'Celtic-Latin Texts in Northern England, c. 1150–c. 1250,' 44. At what point a truncated version of this kind began to circulate is unclear. I can see no reason for postulating a partial recension in Bede's day. There is a strong presumption that he had the entire *De excidio* before him and merely selected those materials pertinent to his depiction. Indeed, I think it likely that what motivated Bede may also have prompted partial transmission of Gildas' text at a later date.

23 Archaeological evidence suggests that substantial numbers of Germanic federates were settled in

Britain well before the mid-fifth century. The traditions regarding Hengist and Horsa may reflect an awareness that the rebellion of Saxon mercenaries in Kent marked an important transition from controlled to uncontrolled settlement: Myres, *Anglo-Saxon Pottery and the Settlement of England*, 95–9.

24 Gildas' attitude is decidedly pro-Roman. The beginnings of the island's troubles stem from an example of British perfidy in their dealings with Rome: DEB, cc 6–7, p 30. Down to the arrival of Hengist and Horsa, Gildas contrasts the Britons with the Romans. Events seem to flow as inevitable consequences from the initial treachery.

25 Dumville dates the Gildasian recension of the *Historia Brittonum* c 1100, and this version of the text appears to have been the most widely used throughout the twelfth century and beyond: Dumville, 'Celtic-Latin Texts in Northern England,' 19. The Sawley manuscript of the *De excidio* offers some very interesting evidence of the confusion which surrounded Gildas' work: ibid, pp 44–6.

26 The handling of Rome's hegemony over the island established a pattern which would be applied to subsequent invading peoples. For medieval writers it was Caesar, not Claudius, who inaugurated the period of Roman domination. The fact that recorded history essentially began with Caesar's expeditions could only underscore the epochal significance which seemed to attach to this juncture in Britain's past.

27 On the historiographic activity in this period see Brooke, 'Historical Writing in England between 850 and 1150,' 223–47; and Gransden, pp 29–91.

28 Robert de Losinga, bishop of Hereford (1079–95), is credited with introducing Marianus' chronicle into England. Bishop Robert himself wrote a tract, in which he elaborated Marianus' objections to the accuracy of the Dionysian era. This work survives, and has been discussed by Stevenson, 'A Contemporary Description of the Domesday Survey,' 72–84. Robert de Losinga was a friend of Wulfstan, the saintly bishop of Worcester (1062–93), and probably gave him a copy of Marianus' universal chronicle. Work began on the *Worcester Chronicle* some time prior to Wulfstan's death in 1095. On the authorship problem and the compilation process see Gransden, pp 145–8.

29 It was this fact which prompted Thorpe to omit the earlier sections from his edition of the *Chronicon ex chronicis*. A more reliable text of the concluding portion is available in *The Chronicle of John of Worcester 1118–1140*, ed Weaver. The only complete edition remains that by William Howard (1592). I should like to thank the Houghton Library, Harvard University, for providing me with a microfilm copy of Howard's edition.

30 The F-redaction is a bilingual version of the *Chronicle*, closely related to E. No complete edition of the F-text has yet been published, though René Derolez has one in preparation. The material from the *Historia Brittonum* occurs in the Latin account of Britain's settlement: *Annales Domitiani Latini*, ed Magoun, pp 243–4. The Domitian Bilingual appears to have been written for Christ Church, Canterbury, c 1100. A similar combination of the *Chronicle* with the *Historia Brittonum* is found in the unpublished *Cronica Imperfecta* also produced at Christ Church. See Dumville, 'The *Liber Floridus* of Lambert of Saint-Omer and the *Historia Brittonum*,' 106.

31 Surprisingly enough, the F-redactor passes over the detailed account of Vortigern's reign (HB, cc 31–49, pp 170–93).

32 Henry of Huntingdon set to work shortly before 1133: Gransden, p 194.

33 The *terminus ante quem* for the *Historia* is 1139, the year in which Henry of Huntingdon saw a copy of the work in Bec. I am inclined to agree with Tatlock that a completion date in mid-1138 seems most plausible, but there is considerable uncertainty. See Tatlock's review of the dating evidence: Tatlock, pp 433–7.

34 Britain simply did not figure in Otto's modified Augustinian viewpoint with its strong Imperial bias. For the concerns of writers at St Denis see: Spiegel, 'The Cult of Saint Denis and Capetian Kingship,' 43–69.

35 See Galbraith, *Historical Research in Medieval England,* 30.

36 The trend is already clear in the *Gesta Stephani.* The author begins with the death of Henry I, which marked England's entry into a time of troubles: *Gesta Stephani,* ed Potter and Davis, 1.1, p 2. At the end of the century Richard of Devizes opens his account with the coronation of Richard I, the dominating force in events after 1189: *The Chronicle of Richard of Devizes of the Time of King Richard the First,* ed Appleby. The examples can easily be multiplied.

37 For example, John of Hexham continued the *Historia regum,* sometimes attributed to Symeon of Durham: *Symeonis monachi Opera omnia,* ed Arnold, 2: 284–332. William of Newburgh explicitly states his intention to treat the period not covered by his predecessors: HRA, 1:19.

38 William takes up these matters in the prologue to his history: HRA, 1:11–19. See Partner, pp 62–8.

39 A notable example of the intrusion of Arthuriana into the affairs of state is Richard's famous gift of the sword Caliburn to Tancred in 1191: *The Chronicle of the Reigns of Henry II. and Richard I., A.D. 1169–1192; Known Commonly under the Name of Benedict of Peterborough,* ed Stubbs, 2:159. The influence of romance on the style of chronicles which deal with contemporary events becomes particularly evident near the close of the century: Gransden, pp 236–42.

40 Wace, *Le Roman de Rou,* ed Holden.

41 The standard studies are Kendrick, *British Antiquity,* and Keeler, *Geoffrey of Monmouth and the Late Latin Chroniclers, 1300–1500.*

42 Both the Vulgate and the Second Variant survive in manuscripts of the twelfth century. Wace drew on the First Variant for his *Roman de Brut,* completed in 1155.

43 Caldwell, 'The Use of Sources in the Variant and Vulgate Versions of the *Historia regum Britanniae* and the Question of the Order of the Versions,' 123–4.

44 The Second Variant survives in fifteen manuscripts, two from the twelfth century. Both Jacob Hammer and Hywel D. Emanuel intended to edit the text, but neither man lived to complete the project. For a list of the manuscripts and a preliminary description of the Second Variant see Emanuel, 'Geoffrey of Monmouth's *Historia regum Britannie*: A Second Variant Version,' 103–10. I have examined microfilm copies of the two twelfth-century manuscripts: Cambridge University Library ms Mm.5.29 and British Library ms Royal 4.C.XI. The post-Arthurian segment of the Second Variant is marked by greater conciseness, but the historical contours remain those of the Vulgate. The substantial divergences from the Vulgate are heavily concentrated in the latter portions of the text, but do not bear on the periodization problem.

45 Hammer knew five manuscripts of the First Variant, two containing the pure variant text (Exeter Cathedral Library ms 3514 and Trinity College, Dublin, ms E.5.12): FV, pp 5–8. Since that time two other manuscripts have been discovered: (1) National Library of Scotland, Edinburgh, ms Adv.18.4.5 (pure). See Cunningham, 74–5; (2) National Library of Wales, Aberystwyth, ms 13210D (conflate). See Huws and Roberts, 147–52. Hammer based his edition not on a manuscript of the pure First Variant, but on the conflate manuscript C (Central Library, Cardiff, ms 2.611). This manuscript has been discussed in detail by Dumville, 'The Origin of the C-Text of the Variant Version of the *Historia regum Britannie*', 315–22. Because the pure and conflate texts diverge so markedly for considerable stretches, Hammer often found it necessary to print the two separately. As a result, I have been able to cite Hammer throughout. A new edition of the First Variant, however, is a prime desideratum.

46 The identifying features of the First Variant will be discussed at length in Chapter 4.

47 In 1929 Acton Griscom and Edmond Faral, each working independently, published editions of

the Standard or Vulgate Version: *The Historia regum Britanniae of Geoffrey of Monmouth*, ed Griscom; Faral's text appeared in his three-volume study *La légende arthurienne*, 3:64–303. Neither man used a sufficiently large group of manuscripts to give one text clear superiority over the other, but Faral's edition does seem to be the better. This text is not divided into books, but Griscom has argued on the basis of the manuscript evidence that in all likelihood such divisions did not originally form part of Geoffrey's *Historia* (Griscom, pp 26–30). The Vulgate Version is cited throughout from Faral's edition, and one can only hope that progress in unravelling the complex textual filiations will someday permit establishment of a truly definitive text.

CHAPTER ONE

1 See Gildas, DEB, c 3, pp 28–9; and Bede, HE, 1.1, pp 14–20. The D, E, and F manuscripts of the *Anglo-Saxon Chronicle* begin in similar fashion: ASC, p 5.
2 A very plausible explanation of what may lie behind Gildas' choice of a starting point has been offered by Stevens, 'Gildas Sapiens,' 355–6.
3 The *Historia Brittonum* dates Brutus' reign by means of a synchronism: 'quando regnabat Britto in Brittannia, Heli sacerdos iudicabat in Israhel et tunc arca testamenti ab alienigenis possidebatur, Postumus frater eius apud Latinos regnabat' (HB, c 11, p 153). Eli's judgeship probably should be placed c 1100 BC, approximately a thousand years before Caesar's expeditions of 55-4 BC (HB, c 19, p 162). The intervening chapters in the *Historia Brittonum* supply legendary materials on the other peoples who inhabit the British Isles. The migration of the Irish out of Scythia is said to have begun at the same time that the children of Israel crossed the Red Sea (HB, c 15, pp 156–7), but such data do not alter the fact that the compiler knows nothing of the Britons' activities between the settlement of the island and Caesar's campaigns. On the importance of the synchronizing tendencies in the *Historia Brittonum* see Dumville, 'On the North British Section of the *Historia Brittonum*,' 349 and 353–4. Dumville has shown conclusively that authorship of this highly composite text can no longer be attributed to Nennius: '"Nennius" and the *Historia Brittonum*,' 78–95. The compilation of the *Historia Brittonum* can be dated with considerable precision to 829–30: Dumville, 'Some Aspects of the Chronology of the *Historia Brittonum*,' 439–40.
4 On the possible reason for passing over Caesar see Stevens, 'Gildas Sapiens,' 355.
5 Molly Miller has contrasted the apparent situation in Britain with that in Herodotus' Greece. The first writers to deal with early Insular history do not seem able to draw upon a comparable corpus of historical and quasi-historical narrative traditions: 'Starting to Write History: Gildas, Bede and Nennius,' 458–9.
6 The tin trade attracted early interest to the area, but little more than rumours appear to have reached writers in the Mediterranean basin: Thomson, *History of Ancient Geography*, 53–6. No eyewitness accounts which antedate Caesar's expeditions have survived, but Pytheas of Marseilles probably journeyed to Britain as much as three centuries earlier. Some of the data gathered on Pytheas' voyage may have found inclusion in later sources: Bunbury, *A History of Ancient Geography*, 1:590–601. See also Thomson, *History of Ancient Geography*, 143–51.
7 Caesar, DBG, 4.20–1, pp 112–14. Despite this precaution, Caesar's lack of familiarity with the coastline and local water conditions resulted in a sizable loss of ships on both expeditions.
8 Jackson, *Language and History in Early Britain*, 96–106.
9 Jackson has shown that a high percentage of the Latin loanwords in Brittonic came from speakers trained in Roman schools: 'On the Vulgar Latin of Roman Britain,' 83–103; and *Language and History in Early Britain*, 107–12. On Gildas' Latin see Kerlouégan, 'Le Latin du *De excidio Britanniae* de Gildas,' 151–76.

10 Caesar is the most important witness to the uses of writing and oral transmission on the Continent: DBG, 6.14, pp 185–6. See Tierney, 'The Celtic Ethnography of Posidonius,' 189–275. Daphne Nash has offered some well-reasoned criticism of Tierney, and sees Caesar as a much more independent authority: 'Reconstructing Poseidonios' Celtic Ethnography: Some Considerations,' 111–26.

11 Chadwick, 'Intellectual Contacts between Britain and Gaul in the Fifth Century,' 189–253.

12 An anonymous 'Gaulish' chronicle was long thought to provide roughly contemporary testimony on the passage of dominion from the Britons to the Anglo-Saxons: Chronica Gallica, ed Mommsen, p 660 (a 441–2). This entry, however, has now been shown to be part of a Carolingian continuation of Jerome: Miller, 'The Last British Entry in the "Gallic Chronicles",' 315–18.

13 Epitoma chronicon, p 472.

14 Nothing is reported beyond the fact that Celestine sent Germanus to Britain. Prosper even leaves the duration of the visit open. Chadwick, however, has pointed out the likelihood that Prosper learned of Germanus' mission in Rome. He is known to have visited the city in 430 and again in 431: Chadwick, Poetry and Letters in Early Christian Gaul, 172. If Prosper did hear news of this campaign against British Pelagians from Roman sources, that would explain the character of the entry and particularly the lack of Insular detail. The possibility also exists that Germanus was still in Britain in 430 and 431, thereby accounting for the absence of any information on how long the mission lasted.

15 Prosper apparently followed Leo I to Rome in 440 immediately following the papal election. Thereafter, Prosper seems to have held a secretarial post in the papal chancellery: Chadwick, Poetry and Letters in Early Christian Gaul, 172–3.

16 Constantius, Vita Germani episcopi Autissiodorensis, ed Levison, cc 12–18, pp 259–65 (first visit); cc 25–7, pp 269–71 (second visit).

17 Vita Germani, cc 17–18, pp 263–5. Levison rightly points out that historical fact has been overlaid with a considerable amount of legend in Constantius' account of the Alleluia Victory: Levison, 'Bischof Germanus von Auxerre und die Quellen zu seiner Geschichte,' 123–4. For a general discussion of Germanus' visits to Britain see de Plinval, 'Les campagnes de saint Germain en Grande-Bretagne contre les Pélagiens,' 135–49.

18 Liber contra collatorem, PL, 51, c 21, col 271.

19 The British Church was, of course, represented at major councils on the Continent during this period. What Prosper appears to mean is direct papal intervention in local ecclesiastical matters.

20 Zosimus, Historia nova, ed Mendelssohn, 6.1–6, pp 282–7. See Thompson, 'Zosimus on the End of Roman Britain,' 163–7.

21 De bello Gothico, ed Haury, 4.20, pp 589–91.

22 See von den Brincken, Studien zur lateinischen Weltchronistik bis in das Zeitalter Ottos von Freising, 108–13.

23 For example, Frechulf of Lisieux treats Augustine's mission as an accomplishment of Gregory's papacy, but no attempt is made to define the conversion's importance for English history: Chronicon, PL, 106, col 1256 (2.5.24). Regino of Prüm handles the material in identical fashion: Chronicon, ed Kurze, a 517–37, p 25. Both writers mention Æthelberht's conversion, but no other Anglo-Saxon king receives notice. The pattern carries through the period and beyond. England's rulers are noted only when their actions have a bearing on major ecclesiastical matters.

24 See for example Frechulf of Lisieux, Chronicon, 2.5.13, cols 1244–5; and Ado of Vienne, Chronicon, PL, 123, cols 101–2 and 105.

25 Only Boniface receives notice in the major histories. His activities as a Continental churchman

and his martyrdom among the Frisians are described in brief. For example, see Ado of Vienne, *Chronicon*, col. 123.

26 The A-text (Parker ms) sporadically includes items bearing on papal history, but beyond these entries only the death of Charlemagne is reported: ASC, a 814, p 39. The E- and F-manuscripts, which contain a great deal of information on Continental affairs, date from after the Norman Conquest.

27 On the intellectual commerce during this period see Levison, *England and the Continent in the Eighth Century*, 132–73.

28 Norman writers did not miss the Roman analogy, but the comparison is with Caesar, not Claudius. Guy of Amiens terms William *Iulius alter: Carmen de Hastingae proelio*, ed Morton and Muntz, line 32, p 4. See also lines 345–54, pp 22–4. William of Poitiers draws an extended parallel with Caesar's expeditions: *Histoire de Guillaume le Conquérant*, ed Foreville, 2.39–40, pp 246–54. William is exceedingly fond of classical analogues. The relationship between Guy's *Carmen* and William's *Gesta Guillelmi* remains unclear.

29 Frutolf of Michelsberg offers perhaps the most extreme example. See his comments on the Norman Conquest: *Chronica*, ed Schmale and Schmale-Ott, p 78. Frutolf provides no other information on post-Conquest Insular affairs. Otto of Freising selects his data using the same criterion of immediate relevance seen earlier. Matilda's marriage to the emperor gives Otto reason to enter some items on Henry I: *Chronica sive Historia de duabus civitatibus*, ed Hofmeister, 7.15, p 329; 7.16, pp 332–3; and 7.21, p 341.

30 Sigebert begins his *Chronographia* with an introductory paragraph on each of the nine peoples whose histories will be traced. He lists the *Angli* as number five, but apparently finds it impossible to treat English history in isolation. The introductory statement begins with the Britons and sketches the events which led up to the Anglo-Saxon conquest: SG, pp 300–1. In the account proper Sigebert regularly includes available data bearing on pre-Saxon Britain. For a discussion of Sigebert's work see von den Brincken, *Studien zur lateinischen Weltchronistik*, 182–7.

31 Jerome omits Caesar's expeditions, and supplies only information bearing directly on Imperial affairs from the Claudian Invasion onwards: *Chronicon*, ed Helm, p 179.

32 Sigebert's entries on Insular affairs reflect the distribution of data in Bede. Though selective, Sigebert does include notices on Anglo-Saxon kings with a consistency not found among earlier Continental writers. See for example (down to Edwin's accession): SG, a 491, p 313; a 561, p 318; a 599, p 320; a 604, p 321; a 615, p 322; and a 616, p 322. This pattern continues until just after the entry on Bede's death (SG, a 731, p 330), when Sigebert states: 'Abhinc regnum Anglorum annotare supersedeo, quia hystorias maiorum, quas sequar, non habeo' (SG, a 735, p 331). The extent of Sigebert's dependence on Bede becomes clear as the account continues. Although items pertaining to English history do not disappear entirely, Sigebert has lost the ability to trace Insular developments.

33 It is difficult to account for Sigebert's handling of these materials, especially since he states that Ambrosius Aurelianus led the British resistance for forty-five years. He has compressed well over a century of Insular history into a single entry. Cf Bede, HE, 1.16, p 54.

34 The encyclopedist Lambert of Saint-Omer would seem to be the first Continental writer to draw on the *Chronicle*. He includes a sizable section on English history in his monumental work completed in 1120: *Liber Floridus*, ed Albert Derolez, fols 68^r–76^r, pp 137–55. Albert Derolez provides a convenient review of the dating evidence in the introduction to the edition, pp vii–viii. The information on English history is drawn in substantial measure from the F-text of the *Anglo-Saxon Chronicle*. For a discussion of Lambert's handling of the sources available to him see René Derolez, 'British and English History in the *Liber Floridus*,' 59–70.

35 Marianus was Irish, but his interest in Bede had nothing to do with this background. From 1056 until his death in 1082 or 1083, Marianus lived on the Continent. The purpose of his universal chronicle was primarily computistical, and he took exception with Bede's system of chronology which had long held sway among Continental writers. The Insular data borrowed from Bede are largely incidental to the discussion of theoretical matters. For an excellent review of Marianus' life and work see von den Brincken, 'Marianus Scottus,' 191–208.

36 Indicative of the problem is the manner in which Lambert of Saint-Omer found it necessary to divide up materials from the *Historia Brittonum*, placing them in several sections of his work. On Lambert's handling of the data see Dumville, 'The *Liber Floridus* of Lambert of Saint-Omer and the *Historia Brittonum*,' 103–22.

37 Henry of Huntingdon set to work compiling the *Historia Anglorum* shortly before 1133. The first edition reached to the year 1129, and a second brought the account down to 1135. This was accomplished by simply extending the final book. No further changes appear to have been made prior to the visit to Bec. In all likelihood it was Henry himself who provided Robert of Torigni with a copy of the *Historia Anglorum* to 1135, presumably the most up-to-date version available at the time. See Gransden, pp 194 and 200.

38 For the later editions and particularly the expanded version (to 1147) see Gransden, p 194; and Partner, pp 17–18.

39 RT, 1:97. The *Epistola ad Warinum* was included by Robert of Torigni in his chronicle, cited here from Delisle's edition. Though extant, Henry of Huntingdon's own text of the letter has not been edited.

40 The information on the origins of the Irish and the Picts is also drawn from the *Historia Brittonum*: HA, 1.9–11, pp 13–16; HB, cc 12–15, pp 154–8.

41 Henry's ignorance of Geoffrey's activities is very puzzling: Tatlock, p 434. The *Historia Anglorum* was written at the behest of Alexander bishop of Lincoln (HA, prologus, p 3), the same man for whom Geoffrey of Monmouth translated the *Prophecies of Merlin* (HRB, cc 109–10, pp 189–90). The two authors obviously moved in similar circles, and Geoffrey certainly knew the *Historia Anglorum*. These curious circumstances prompted Brooke's contention that Henry of Huntingdon was 'evidently singled out to be one of the first and most considerable victims of the fraud:' Brooke, 'The Archbishops of St David's, Llandaff and Caerleon-on-Usk,' 231. Although I can see no reason for such trickery, Brooke's view is a possibility. Even if Geoffrey did purposely conceal the existence of his work from Henry, the success of this deception only underscores the importance of chance, where historical research in the twelfth century was concerned. For the context of Henry's visit to Bec see Saltmann, *Theobald, Archbishop of Canterbury*, 14–15.

42 GRA, prologus, 1:1–3. Æthelweard was not widely known; indeed, no other writer can be shown to have had firsthand familiarity with the text until the sixteenth century: Campbell, ÆC, p ix. William of Malmesbury boasts that he is the first since Bede to treat the whole of English history in Latin, thereby discounting Æthelweard entirely: GRA, prologus, 1:1. On the date of Æthelweard's chronicle see Campbell, ÆC, pp xii–xvi.

43 HRB, c 208, p 303. The Second Variant also contains the full epilogue: CUL, ms Mm. 5.29, fol. 107^r and BL, ms Royal 4.C.XI, fol. 248^v. The First Variant has a much shorter version which omits the names of the three historians: 'Regum autem acta qui ab illo tempore in Gwaliis successerunt et fortunas successoribus meis scribendas dimitto, ego Galfridus Arturus Monemuthensis, qui hanc historiam Britonum de eorum lingua in nostram transferre curavi' (FV, 11.18, p 264). On the use made of Caradoc's name in the epilogue see Tatlock, p 5.

44 The fact that so many later writers saw Merlin's prophecies fulfilled in events of their own day bears witness to the correctness of Geoffrey's supposition. On the structure and function of the

vaticinations see Pähler, *Strukturuntersuchungen zur 'Historia regum Britanniae' des Geoffrey of Monmouth,* 127–49.

45 Henry describes his efforts in the *Epistola ad Warinum,* RT, 1:97.

46 On the rhythm of the narrative see Pähler, *Strukturuntersuchungen,* 87–126.

47 See Faral, 2:70–81.

48 Prior to their Continental campaign Belinus and Brennius, the sons of Dunvallo Molmutius, wage war against each other until a reconciliation is brought about by their mother: HRB, cc 35–41, pp 108–15.

49 Brennus' campaign is reported in many sources. For example, see Orosius, HAP, 2.19, pp 130–1.

50 Faral is persuaded that Geoffrey altered the name slightly from Brennus to Brennius in order to mask the borrowing of such a well-attested figure (Faral, 2:135). Tatlock, on the other hand, feels that Geoffrey wanted to demonstrate the superiority of his knowledge (Tatlock, p 169, fn 279). Although Tatlock is undoubtedly much closer to the truth, he misses the importance which attaches to providing partial corroboration for such a crucial juncture in British history.

51 The *Annales* were begun in 1143 (Tatlock, pp 210–11, and Gransden, p 212). The completion date cannot be fixed with any certainty because Alfred does not carry the account down to his own day. The last events recorded are those for the year 1129. Hearne added the title *Annales* (AB, p 1, fn 1), which is something of a misnomer. Strictly speaking, the arrangement of materials does not become annalistic until rather late in the account (AB, p 99).

52 Remarking Alfred's inconsistency on the question of corroborating testimony, Tatlock terms him a 'dullard' (Tatlock, p 210). This judgment is excessively harsh and betrays a lack of understanding for the problems faced by Alfred. The beginnings of a more just evaluation have been provided by Hammer, 'Note on a Manuscript of Geoffrey of Monmouth's *Historia regum Britanniae,'* 225–34.

53 Alfred divides his account of British rule into five unequal sections, the *quinque status regni.* Each of the first five books treats a separate *status.* Use of this structural device ends with the passage of dominion.

54 Alfred remarks: 'Horum gesta tam Romana quam Britania narrat hystoria, de quibus hic aliqua sunt memoranda' (AB, p 16). Belinus' deeds, however, are not recounted in Roman sources, and this statement must be regarded as an empty formula.

55 On Robert's life and historiographic activity see Gransden, pp 261–3.

56 This feature of Geoffrey's *Historia* is emphasized by Hanning, *The Vision of History in Early Britain,* 123.

57 Geoffrey inserts ten synchronisms into his account: HRB, c 22, p 92; c 25, p 96; c 26, p 96; c 27, p 97; c 28, p 98; c 29, p 98; c 30, pp 98–9; c 32, p 106; c 64, p 138; c 68, p 141. See the discussion of the first eight synchronisms in Parry, 'The Chronology of Geoffrey of Monmouth's *Historia,* Books I and II,' 316–22.

58 See Delisle's discussion of the manuscript transmission: RT, 1:iii–liii.

59 Delisle prints separately all the interpolations made by Robert in Eusebius-Jerome and Sigebert. For the period before 381 see RT, 1:1–3.

60 Æthelweard's chronicle is a case in point. By treating the Anglo-Saxons in this context, he implies their importance for the larger structures of history. Æthelweard dedicated the chronicle to his relative Matilda of Essen: ÆC, p 1. She was the granddaughter of the Emperor Otto I and his wife Edith, Athelstan's sister. Æthelweard obviously intended his approach to instil in Matilda a sense of pride in her Anglo-Saxon heritage.

61 These interpolations are printed separately by Delisle, RT, 1:3–6.

62 See Gransden, pp 195–200.

63 See Gransden, p 194; and Partner, pp 17–18.

64 I regard Geoffrey's old book as a topos, although the tantalizing possibility that such a source once existed continues to attract believers. For example, see Southern, 'Aspects of the European Tradition of Historical Writing, 1. The Classical Tradition from Einhard to Geoffrey of Monmouth,' 194.

65 In the prologue to his chronicle Jerome comments on the need to add Roman data to Eusebius' account: *Chronicon*, p 6.

66 In Books 2–4 (from Caesar to the appeal to Aetius) Alfred's style becomes that of the compiler, not the epitomist: AB, pp 24–46. Material from other sources, principally Bede, is inserted wherever available; indeed, for some sections the *Historia ecclesiastica* provides the underlying framework, Geoffrey the supplemental data.

67 Hengist has his daughter Renwein brought over from the Continent. She blinds Vortigern with passion, and Hengist receives Kent in return for his consent to their marriage: HRB, c 100, pp 178–9.

68 Geoffrey derived the nucleus of the story from the *Historia Brittonum* (HB, cc 40–2, pp 181–6).

69 Geoffrey does not date the first landing with any precision. After describing Vortigern's fear that both the Picts and the rightful heirs might launch attacks, it is simply stated: 'Interea applicuerunt tres ciullae, quas longas naves dicimus, in partibus Cantiae, plenae armatis militibus, quibus duo fratres, Horsus et Hengistus, ducatum praestabant' (HRB, c 98, p 175).

CHAPTER TWO

1 The *Anglo-Saxon Chronicle* was the principal source of information on the early English kingdoms. Bede devoted no space to their significance for the Germanic take-over. Down to the twelfth century the *Anglo-Saxon Chronicle* did not spread beyond Britain's shores, and the importance attached to the kingdoms constituted a uniquely Insular perception of what had transpired.

2 For example, see the entries in the Parker ms on events during the second half of the fifth century: *Two of the Saxon Chronicles Parallel*, ed Plummer, 1:12–14. Many of the place names mentioned cannot now be identified, and it must be assumed that medieval writers also found at least some of the battle sites obscure. This would further cloud the question of territorial control.

3 Although Caesar's information is limited, he regularly speaks of Britain's tribes in the plural, and does provide some specific data. After Mandubracius treats with Caesar on behalf of the Trinovantes (DBG, 5.20, p 142), five other tribes submit: the Cenimagni, the Segontiaci, the Ancalites, the Bibroci, and the Cassi (DBG, 5.21, p 142). Kent is also said to be ruled by four kings (DBG, 5.22, p 142). Gildas provides far less material, but he always uses the plural forms *reges* and *tyranni* when discussing British rule in general. He does supply the names of five corrupt kings and specifies the territory controlled by two of them: DEB, cc 27–33, pp 41–4.

4 See for example Orosius' account of Caesar's two expeditions: HAP, 6.9, pp 377–9. Bede, of course, follows Orosius for these campaigns (HE, 1.2, pp 20–2) and omits the specific information on sixth-century British rule found in Gildas.

5 The compiler rarely specifies the names and locations of Celtic realms, but a large number of British kings are mentioned: HB, cc 62–4, pp 205–8.

6 For example, Belinus and Brennius conquer Rome only after the cessation of hostilities between them (HRB, cc 35–44, pp 108–18). Cassibellaunus also enjoys great success against Caesar so long as the Britons remain united (HRB, cc 54–63, pp 126–37). The consequences of internal strife are clear throughout the account.

7 That would seem to be the function of Merlin's prophecies. See Pähler, *Strukturuntersuchungen*,

136–49. Geoffrey's methods are often playful and sometimes downright mischievous; indeed, Brooke has convincingly argued for the presence of parodistic elements in the *Historia*: Brooke, 'Geoffrey of Monmouth as a Historian,' 77–91. I do not, however, regard this feature of the work as incompatible with a fundamentally serious didactic intent. It seems to me that Flint goes much too far in elaborating upon Brooke's very useful insight: Flint, 'The *Historia regum Britanniae* of Geoffrey of Monmouth,' 447–68.

8 Schirmer, *Die frühen Darstellungen des Arthurstoffes*, 23–8.

9 Among contemporary writers Geoffrey's concerns are hardly unusual. For example, William of Malmesbury also attaches significance to strong, centralized rule: Gluckauf Haahr, 'The Concept of Kingship in William of Malmesbury's *Gesta regum* and *Historia novella*,' 351–71.

10 For a thorough discussion of what is known about these kings see O'Sullivan, pp 87–133.

11 Constantine is said to rule over Damnonia (DEB, c 28, p 41), Vortiporius over Demetia (DEB, c 31, p 43).

12 Collingwood and Myres, *Roman Britain and the English Settlements*, 313–15. See also Jackson, *Language and History in Early Britain*, 115–16.

13 The entries in question are appended to Anglo-Saxon genealogies: HB, cc 57–66, pp 202–9.

14 See Dumville, 'Sub-Roman Britain: History and Legend,' 177.

15 See the annals for 516 and 537: *Annales Cambriae*, p 154.

16 The reason given for the campaign is the pressing need for financial reserves, but consolidation is the real issue. Without sufficient funds Arthur could not hope to maintain his position.

17 This is consistent with the manner in which Geoffrey evaluates British achievement throughout the *Historia*.

18 Faral attributes the milder tone of the *Historia* to a desire on Geoffrey's part to place the rulers in a somewhat more favourable light: Faral, 2:312. I am prepared to accept that Cuneglasus' omission may stem from the heinous nature of his transgressions, but Faral does not take the very real stylistic differences sufficiently into account.

19 William of Newburgh had seen a copy of the *De excidio* some years earlier, but apparently did not have the text in front of him when he composed his denunciation of Geoffrey. William recalls only the style and general thrust of Gildas' work: HRA, 1:11.

20 Geoffrey mentions a Cerdic among the Saxon leaders when the second wave of Continental invaders puts ashore in Britain (HRB, c 101, p 180). This figure probably should be identified with Cerdic, the legendary founder of the kingdom of Wessex (Tatlock, p 147). The name also occurs twice in the *Historia Brittonum*: (1) as the name of Vortigern's interpreter (HB, c 37, p 177), and (2) as the name of the British king of Elmet in Edwin's day (HB, c 63, p 206. See also Bede, HE, 4.23, p 410). The latter seems to be the king whose death is recorded in the *Annales Cambriae*, p 157 (annal for 616).

21 A twelfth-century fragment of a *chanson de geste* dealing with Gormund's Continental career and his death is extant: *Gormont et Isembart: Fragment de chanson de geste du XIIe siècle*, ed Bayot. The events, however, are set in the ninth century, not the late sixth (Faral, 2:312–13). Geoffrey's *Historia* and the fragment offer the earliest evidence of this narrative tradition. How to account for the chronological discrepancy is a matter for speculation.

22 The poem fragment contains a reference to the siege of Cirencester, placed in the mouth of Isembart: *Gormont et Isembart*, line 472, p 33. Despite discrepancies in the chronology, the *chanson de geste* seems to be the Continental sequel to Insular events recounted by Geoffrey.

23 Abbot Dinoot of the monastery at Bangor enunciates the position of the British Church. Geoffrey describes a confrontation between Augustine and Dinoot in which the latter's arguments are said to have prevailed (HRB, c 188, p 284). This section is obviously the Galfridian counterpart to the meeting at Augustine's Oak depicted by Bede (HE, 2.2, pp 134–6).

24 Faral argues that behind the tripartite division of the Saxon domain lie Northumbria, Mercia, and Wessex, the three kingdoms which would gain ascendancy (Faral, 2:310). The hegemonies in question, however, are successive, not simultaneous. Faral is well aware of this fact, and I find his suggestion interesting though somewhat forced.

25 Geoffrey consistently refers to the Anglo-Saxons as *Saxones*, but Pope Gregory sends Augustine 'ut Anglis verbum Dei praedicaret' (HRB, c 188, p 283). Tatlock is doubtless correct in connecting this abrupt shift in usage with Bede's sudden importance as Geoffrey's principal source (Tatlock, p 19). Cf Bede, HE, 1.23, p 68.

26 The image of Æthelfrith, the fierce Northumbrian king, comes from Bede (HE, 2.2, pp 140–2). In Geoffrey's account, however, Æthelfrith is incited against the Britons by Æthelberht (HRB, c 189, p 284). The king of Kent is made to bear part of the blame for the slaughter at Chester, as once again Geoffrey casts a somewhat different light on events recounted by Bede.

27 There is some uncertainty in the Vulgate manuscripts regarding the duration of the British campaign of guerrilla warfare. Irrespective of the number given, however, a considerable time-lag remains between the Britons' loss of name and Athelstan's accession. Geoffrey's didactic construct depends upon the separation itself and not on the precise number of years. Cf Griscom, p 535.

28 Hunter Blair, *An Introduction to Anglo-Saxon England*, 87.

29 Hunter Blair cautions that, although Athelstan may loom large in the eyes of posterity, the accuracy of such a view is questionable: *An Introduction to Anglo-Saxon England*, 87–9. Athelstan's achievements did not long survive his passing.

CHAPTER THREE

1 Down through the Battle of Mount Badon Bede's depiction rests on a Gildasian base, but Henry of Huntingdon did not know the *De excidio*. In the *Historia Anglorum* Gildas is cited as the putative source of Arthur's twelve victories (HA, 2.18, p 49). This passage attests to Henry's confusion regarding the work upon which Gildas' reputation as a historian rested. The mistaken attribution probably stems from Henry's use of the Gildasian recension of the *Historia Brittonum*.

2 See Partner, pp 22–5 and 27–8.

3 Bede takes up the background for the mission following his brief sketch of the British decline in the wake of Mount Badon: HE, 1.22, pp 66–8.

4 In the *Historia Anglorum* the first landing is assigned to the traditional date, 449: HA, 2.1, p 38.

5 It is not completely certain in what form Henry found the *Historia regum Britanniae* at Bec. To judge from the letter to Warin, however, the underlying regnal list agreed substantially with the three principal recensions, and that fact suffices for the present discussion.

6 Henry's borrowings are so slight as to leave frequent uncertainty regarding the interrelationship between the texts. For an indisputable example of Henry's dependence on Geoffrey see Tatlock, p 49.

7 Her excellent discussion leaves no doubt of the extent to which the *contemptus mundi* theme informed Henry's writings: Partner, pp 33–40.

8 The concluding segments of the work are extant, and Gaimar himself states that 'Il començat la u Jasun / Ala conquere la tuisun' (EdE, lines 6523–4, p 206).

9 See Bell, EdE, p ix; and Williamson, 'Ralf son of Gilbert and Ralf son of Ralf,' 19–27.

10 Gaimar states: 'Gaimar i mist Marz e Averil / E tuz les dusze mais, / Ainz k'il oust translaté des reis' (EdE, lines 6432–4, p 204). Bell (p lii) takes these lines to mean that the entire history was compiled over a fourteen-month period. Although Tatlock (p 452) is not certain that Gaimar should be interpreted literally, he does feel that the work was composed rapidly.

11 See EDE, lines 401–15, p 13; and lines 503–26, p 16.

12 Bell has advanced this hypothesis: EDE, p xii.

13 Bell, 'The "Prologue" to Gaimar,' 170–5.

14 In the H-manuscript (College of Arms, London, ms Arundel XIV) the prologue has been dropped. The Haveloc story appears after the *Estoire des Engleis* in a somewhat different form: *Le Lai d'Haveloc*, ed Bell. The *Estoire des Engleis* itself begins with Cerdic's arrival (EDE, line 817, p 25).

15 'Gaimar's Early "Danish" Kings,' 619.

16 When Arthur invaded Denmark, Haveloc's father King Guntier fell in battle. Fearing for the life of the rightful heir, Guntier's widow fled by sea with her young son Haveloc. The ship, however, came to grief on the coast of Britain, and the queen died. Haveloc then grew up a kitchen boy, unaware of both his royal ancestry and his name. The background is subsequently made known to Haveloc: EDE, lines 401–15, p 13; and lines 503–26, p 16.

17 Gaimar describes the extent of their territorial holdings in some detail: EDE, lines 45–52, p 2.

18 See my forthcoming article: '*Se ço est veir que Gilde dit*: Gaimar, Gildas, and Geoffrey of Monmouth.'

19 Bell, 'Gaimar's Early "Danish" Kings,' 638.

20 Bell is persuaded that Gaimar reached lines 1592–1612, p 51, before interpolating the Haveloc story and the Wasing episode: 'Gaimar's Early "Danish" Kings,' 620.

21 The *Annales* were begun during a period of enforced idleness. Alfred states that in consequence of a decree promulgated at the Council of London the 'multitude of excommunicates' forced suspension of divine office in his church (AB, pp 1–2). The reference would appear to be to the legatine council in mid-Lent 1143, presided over by Henry of Blois, bishop of Winchester: Gransden, p 212. See also Tatlock, pp 210–11.

22 The use of Gormund's Donation to mark the passage of dominion is also a feature of the First Variant: FV, 11.7, p 254. The anonymous redactor, however, uses the renaming of the island to underscore the advent of a new era, not the Britons' name change. There is every reason to believe that Alfred had no precedent, but rather worked independently, using a copy of the Vulgate.

23 The prefatory list enumerates the kingdoms in the following order: Kent, Sussex, Wessex, Essex, East Anglia, Mercia, and Northumbria (HA, 1.4, pp 8–9). The chronological sequence of the foundings is Kent (HA, 2.4, p 41), Sussex (HA, 2.8 and 2.10, p 44), Wessex (HA, 2.16, p 47), Essex (HA, 2.19, pp 49–50), Northumbria (HA, 2.21, p 50), East Anglia (HA, 2.25, pp 52–3), and Mercia (HA, 2.26, p 53).

24 Although dates are not assigned to the founding of East Anglia (HA, 2.25, pp 52–3) and Mercia (HA, 2.26, p 53), the entries in which these events are discussed fall after Æthelberht's accession (HA, 2.23, p 51).

25 Bede is the only authority mentioned by name in the prologue (AB, p 3), and Alfred does indeed attach considerable importance to the *Historia ecclesiastica*.

26 Alfred uses the *Historia ecclesiastica* most heavily in Books 2–4: AB, pp 24–46.

27 Levison first drew attention to this manuscript: 'A Combined Manuscript of Geoffrey of Monmouth and Henry of Huntingdon,' 41–51. See now Dumville, 'The Origin of the C-Text,' 316–19.

28 For a convenient survey of Gervase's life and works see Gransden, pp 253–60.

29 Some sense of the importance which Christ Church assumed in Gervase's writings generally can be seen from the tracts prefixed to the *Chronica*: GC, 1:3–83.

30 In his *Mappa mundi* Gervase asserts that if British buildings had survived, they would have proved the truth of the *Historia regum Britanniae*: GC, 2:414.

31 RD, 1:296–7; 2:64; 2:67; 2:163. See the additional example in a separate work which lists the bishops of Lincoln: RD, 2:202. Cf Gransden, p 235.

32 On Ralph Diceto's life and works see Gransden, pp 230–6. Stubbs' discussion of the manuscripts remains the standard: RD, 1:lxxxviii–xcvi.

33 Two rather obvious examples will suffice: (1) Guithelinus' journey to Brittany, the restoration of the British monarchy under Constantine, and the names of Constantine's sons are all reported (RD, 1:80); (2) Arthur's conquest of Gaul is also noted (RD, 1:91). A substantial number of lesser borrowings can also be found.

34 Stubbs has printed these interpolations in his apparatus at the bottom of each page.

35 For the few facts known about Roger of Wendover see Gransden, pp 359–60.

36 The Coxe edition starts with Roger's account of events leading up to Vortigern's invitation. For the earlier portions of the *Flores historiarum* consult the first volume of Luard's edition of Matthew Paris' *Chronica majora*. Matthew made the *Flores historiarum* the basis for his own account. Roger's text is printed in small type to differentiate it from Matthew's interpolations.

CHAPTER FOUR

1 Caldwell, 'Wace's *Roman de Brut* and the *Variant Version* of Geoffrey of Monmouth's *Historia regum Britanniae*,' 675–82.

2 Gallais, 'La *Variant Version* de l'*Historia regum Britanniae* et le *Brut* de Wace,' 1–32.

3 On the supplemental use of Bede in the First Variant see Hammer, FV, pp 11–12; and Caldwell, 'The Use of Sources,' 123–4.

4 There is another fairly prominent Athelstan, the ninth-century king of Kent, but I fail to see how the information available on this figure could have given rise to the confusion: ASC, a 839, p 41; and a 851, pp 42–3.

5 The Vulgate reads: 'Degenerati autem a britannica nobilitate, Gualenses nunquam postea monarchiam insulae recuperaverunt, immo nunc sibi, interdum Saxonibus ingrati consurgentes, externas atque domesticas clades incessanter agebant' (HRB, c 207, p 303).

6 Hammer discussed this feature of the c-text to illustrate the conflation process: FV, pp 15–16.

7 From Merlin's prophecy on Vortigern's death through to the end, Hammer repeatedly found it necessary to print the texts of individual manuscripts or groups of manuscripts separately. The divergences simply became too great from c, on which the edition is based. Aurelius Ambrosius' return from Brittany marks the end of the substantial agreement between the various manuscripts: FV, 8.1, p 135.

8 Tatlock (pp 456–62) provides a convenient survey of these fragments. The texts must be dated on the basis of linguistic evidence; hence the uncertainty.

9 Following the preview of the name change, the island is often designated *Engleterre* (down to the end of the account): RdB, line 13,420, p 700; line 13,421, p 701; line 13,649, p 714; line 13,650, p 714 (*Englelande*); line 13,838, p 724; line 14,241, p 745; line 14,247, p 745; line 14,352, p 751; line 14,707, p 770; line 14,759, p 773; and line 14,787, p 775.

10 See Houck, *Sources of the 'Roman de Brut' of Wace*, 261–87.

11 Holden discusses this point in the introduction to his edition of the *Roman de Rou*, 3:108–10.

12 Drawing on the Vulgate, Wace adds the tale of Brian and the venison omitted in the First Variant: RdB, lines 14,186–222, pp 742–4; HRB, c 193, p 290. See Caldwell, 'Wace's *Roman de Brut* and the *Variant Version*,' 681.

13 The First Variant does state that the Anglo-Saxons who overran the island introduced laws *de terra sua*, presumably their Continental homeland and so interpreted by Wace: FV, 11.16, p 263.

14 The *Roman de Brut* echoes the wording of the First Variant: 'Creati sunt interea plurimi reges Anglorum Saxonum, qui in diversis partibus Loegriae regnaverunt' (FV, 11.8, p 254).
15 Layamon does not identify the kingdoms.
16 Layamon adds the famous story of Pope Gregory's encounter with English slaves (LB, lines 14,695–720, pp 768–70), but does not otherwise alter the contours of Wace's account, even though many points are elaborated.

WORKS CITED

I PRIMARY SOURCES

Ado of Vienne *Chronicon* Patrologiae Cursus Completus: Series Latina (Migne), 123, cols 23–138

Æthelweard *Chronicon* ed A. Campbell Nelson's Medieval Texts (Edinburgh 1962)

Alfred of Beverley *Annales, sive Historia de gestis regum Britanniae* ed Thomas Hearne (Oxford 1716)

The Anglo-Saxon Chronicle: A Revised Translation ed Dorothy Whitelock with David C. Douglas and Susie I. Tucker (London 1961)

Annales Cambriae ed Egerton Phillimore *Y Cymmrodor*, 9 (1888), 152–69

Annales Domitiani Latini ed Francis P. Magoun, Jr *Mediaeval Studies*, 9 (1947), 235–95

Bede *Ecclesiastical History of the English People* ed Bertram Colgrave and R.A.B. Mynors Oxford Medieval Texts (Oxford 1969)

Caesar, C. Julius *De bello Gallico* ed Otto Seel *Commentarii rerum gestarum*, 1 (Leipzig 1961)

Chronica Gallica ed Theodor Mommsen Monumenta Germaniae Historica: Auctores Antiquissimi, 9 (Berlin 1892) 615–66

The Chronicle of the Reigns of Henry II. and Richard I., A.D. 1169–1192; Known Commonly Under the Name of Benedict of Peterborough ed William Stubbs 2 vols Rolls Series (London 1867)

Chronicon ex chronicis [Worcester Chronicle] ed William Howard (London 1592)

— ed Benjamin Thorpe 2 vols (1848–9; repr Vaduz 1964)

Constantius *Vita Germani episcopi Autissiodorensis* ed W. Levison Monumenta Germaniae Historica: Scriptores Rerum Merovingicarum, 7/1 (Hannover and Leipzig 1919) 225–83

Diceto, Ralph *The Historical Works* ed William Stubbs 2 vols Rolls Series (London 1876)

Eutropius *Breviarium* ed H. Droysen Monumenta Germaniae Historica: Auctores Antiquissimi, 2 (Berlin 1879)

Frechulf of Lisieux *Chronicon* Patrologiae Cursus Completus: Series Latina (Migne), 106, cols 917–1258

Frutolf of Michelsberg *Chronica* ed Franz-Josef Schmale and Irene Schmale-Ott Ausgewählte Quellen zur deutschen Geschichte des Mittelalters: Freiherr vom Stein-Gedächtnisausgabe, 15 (Darmstadt 1972)

Gaimar, Geffrei *L'Estoire des Engleis* ed Alexander Bell Anglo-Norman Texts, 14–16 (Oxford 1960)

Geoffrey of Monmouth *Historia regum Britanniae* ed Edmond Faral *La légende arthurienne*, 3 Bibliothèque de l'École des Hautes Études, Sciences historiques et philologiques, 257 (Paris 1929) 64–303

— *Historia regum Britanniae* ed Acton Griscom (London, New York and Toronto 1929)

— *Historia regum Britanniae: A Variant Version* ed Jacob Hammer Publications of the Mediaeval Academy of America, 57 (Cambridge, Mass. 1951)

— *Historia regum Britanniae* [Second Variant] British Library MS Royal 4.C.XI, fols 222–49

— *Historia regum Britanniae* [Second Variant] Cambridge University Library MS Mm.5.29, fols 20–106

Gervase of Canterbury *The Historical Works* ed William Stubbs 2 vols Rolls Series (London 1879–80)

Gesta Stephani ed K.R. Potter and R.H.C. Davis 2nd ed Oxford Medieval Texts (Oxford 1976)

Gildas *De excidio et conquestu Britanniae* ed Theodor Mommsen Monumenta Germaniae Historica: Auctores Antiquissimi, 13 (Berlin 1898) 25–85

Gormont et Isembart: Fragment de chanson de geste du XIIe siècle ed Alphonse Bayot 2nd ed Classiques Français du Moyen Âge (Paris 1921)

Guy of Amiens *Carmen de Hastingae proelio* ed Catherine Morton and Hope Muntz Oxford Medieval Texts (Oxford 1972)

Henry of Huntingdon *Epistola ad Warinum* ed Léopold Delisle *Chronique de Robert de Torigni*, 1 (Rouen 1872) 97–111

— *Historia Anglorum* ed Thomas Arnold Rolls Series (London 1879)

Historia Brittonum ed Theodor Mommsen Monumenta Germaniae Historica: Auctores Antiquissimi, 13 (Berlin 1898) 111–222

Jerome *Chronicon* ed Rudolf Helm 2nd ed *Eusebius Werke*, 7 Die griechischen christlichen Schriftsteller der ersten Jahrhunderte, 47 (Berlin 1956)

John of Worcester *The Chronicle of John of Worcester 1118–1140, Being the Continuation of the 'Chronicon ex chronicis' of Florence of Worcester* ed J.R.H. Weaver

John of Worcester *The Chronicle of John of Worcester 1118–1140, Being the Continuation of the 'Chronicon ex chronicis' of Florence of Worcester* ed J.R.H. Weaver

Anecdota Oxoniensia, Mediaeval and Modern Series, 13 (Oxford 1908)
Le Lai d'Haveloc ed Alexander Bell Publications of the University of Manchester, French
Series, 4 (Manchester 1925)
Lambert of Saint-Omer Liber Floridus ed Albert Derolez (Ghent 1968)
Layamon Brut ed G. L. Brook and R. F. Leslie 2 vols Early English Text Society, 250, 277
(Oxford 1963–78)
Notitia dignitatum ed Otto Seeck (Berlin 1876)
Orosius, Paulus Historiarum adversum paganos libri VII ed C. Zangemeister Corpus
Scriptorum Ecclesiasticorum Latinorum, 5 (1882; repr Hildesheim 1967)
Otto of Freising Chronica sive Historia de duabus civitatibus ed A. Hofmeister 2nd ed
Monumenta Germaniae Historica: Scriptores Rerum Germanicarum in usum scholar-
um, 45 (Hannover and Leipzig 1912)
Paris, Matthew Chronica majora ed H. R. Luard 7 vols Rolls Series (London 1872–83)
Procopius De bello Gothico ed Jakob Haury Procopii Caesariensis Opera Omnia, 2
(Leipzig 1963)
Prosper of Aquitaine Epitoma chronicon ed Theodor Mommsen Monumenta Germaniae
Historica: Auctores Antiquissimi, 9 (Berlin 1892) 341–499
— Liber contra collatorem Patrologiae Cursus Completus: Series Latina (Migne), 51,
cols 213–76
Regino of Prüm Chronicon ed F. Kurze Monumenta Germaniae Historica: Scriptores
Rerum Germanicarum, 50 (Hannover 1890)
Richard of Devizes The Chronicle of Richard of Devizes of the Time of King Richard the
First ed John T. Appleby Nelson's Medieval Texts (Edinburgh 1963)
Robert of Torigni Chronique ed Léopold Delisle 2 vols (Rouen 1872–3)
Roger of Wendover Chronica, sive Flores historiarum ed H. O. Coxe 4 vols. (London
1841–2)
Sigebert of Gembloux Chronographia ed L. C. Bethmann Monumenta Germaniae
Historica: Scriptores, 6 (1844; repr Leipzig 1925) 268–374
Two of the Saxon Chronicles Parallel ed Charles Plummer 2 vols (Oxford 1892–9)
Wace Le Roman de Brut ed Ivor Arnold 2 vols Société des Anciens Textes Français (Paris
1938–40)
— Le Roman de Rou ed A. J. Holden 3 vols Société des Anciens Textes Français (Paris
1970–3)
William of Malmesbury Gesta regum Anglorum ed William Stubbs 2 vols Rolls Series
(London 1887–9)
William of Newburgh Historia rerum Anglicarum ed Richard Howlett 2 vols
Chronicles of the Reigns of Stephen, Henry II. and Richard I., 1–2 Rolls Series (London
1884–5)
William of Poitiers Histoire de Guillaume le Conquérant ed Raymonde Foreville Les

Classiques de l'Histoire de France au Moyen Âge (Paris 1952)
Zosimus *Historia nova* ed Ludwig Mendelssohn (1887; repr Hildesheim 1963)

II SECONDARY SOURCES

Atkinson, Donald *'Classis Britannica' Historical Essays in Honour of James Tait* eds J.G. Edwards, V.H. Galbraith, and E.F. Jacob (Manchester 1933) 1–11
Bell, Alexander 'Gaimar's Early "Danish" Kings' *Publications of the Modern Language Association of America*, 65 (1950) 601–40
— 'The "Prologue" to Gaimar' *Modern Language Review*, 15 (1920) 170–5
Brincken, Anna-Dorothee von den 'Marianus Scottus: Unter besonderer Berücksichtigung der nicht veröffentlichten Teile seiner Chronik' *Deutsches Archiv für Erforschung des Mittelalters*, 17 (1961) 191–238
— *Studien zur lateinischen Weltchronistik bis in das Zeitalter Ottos von Freising* (Düsseldorf 1957)
Brooke, Christopher 'The Archbishops of St David's, Llandaff and Caerleon-on-Usk' *Studies in the Early British Church* ed Nora K. Chadwick (Cambridge 1958) 201–42
— 'Geoffrey of Monmouth as a Historian' *Church and Government in the Middle Ages: Essays Presented to C.R. Cheney on his 70th Birthday* eds C.N.L. Brooke, D.E. Luscombe, G.H. Martin, and Dorothy Owen (Cambridge 1976) 76–91
— 'Historical Writing in England between 850 and 1150' *La storiografia altomedievale*, 1, Settimane di studio del Centro italiano di studi sull'alto medioevo, 17/1 (Spoleto 1970) 223–47
Bunbury, E.H. *A History of Ancient Geography* 2nd ed 2 vols (New York 1959)
Caldwell, Robert A. 'The Use of Sources in the Variant and Vulgate Versions of the *Historia regum Britanniae* and the Question of the Order of the Versions' *Bulletin Bibliographique de la Société Internationale Arthurienne*, 9 (1957) 123–4
— 'Wace's *Roman de Brut* and the *Variant Version* of Geoffrey of Monmouth's *Historia regum Britanniae*' *Speculum*, 31 (1956) 675–82
Chadwick, Nora K. 'Intellectual Contacts between Britain and Gaul in the Fifth Century' *Studies in Early British History* ed Nora K. Chadwick (Cambridge 1954) 189–253
— *Poetry and Letters in Early Christian Gaul* (London 1955)
Collingwood, R.G. and Myres, J.N.L. *Roman Britain and the English Settlements* 2nd ed (Oxford 1937)
Cunningham, I.C. 'National Library of Scotland, Edinburgh, MS Adv. 18.4.5' *Scriptorium*, 27 (1973) 74–5
Derolez, René 'British and English History in the *Liber Floridus*' *'Liber Floridus' Colloquium: Papers Read at the International Meeting Held in the University Library Ghent on 3–5 September 1967* ed Albert Derolez (Ghent 1973) 59–70

Dumville, David N. 'The Anglian Collection of Royal Genealogies and Regnal Lists'
Anglo-Saxon England, 5 (1976) 23–50
— 'Celtic-Latin Texts in Northern England, c. 1150 – c. 1250' *Celtica*, 12 (1977) 19–49
— 'Kingship, Genealogies and Regnal Lists' *Early Medieval Kingship* eds P.H. Sawyer
and I.N. Wood (Leeds 1977) 72–104
— 'The *Liber Floridus* of Lambert of Saint-Omer and the *Historia Brittonum*' *Bulletin
of the Board of Celtic Studies*, 26 (1974–6) 103–22
— ' "Nennius" and the *Historia Brittonum*' *Studia Celtica*, 10–11 (1975–6) 78–95
— 'On the North British Section of the *Historia Brittonum*' *Welsh History Review*, 8
(1977) 345–54
— 'The Origin of the c-Text of the Variant Version of the *Historia regum Britanniae*'
Bulletin of the Board of Celtic Studies, 26 (1974–6) 315–22
— 'Some Aspects of the Chronology of the *Historia Brittonum*' *Bulletin of the Board of
Celtic Studies*, 25 (1972–4) 439–45
— 'Sub-Roman Britain: History and Legend' *History*, 62 (1977) 173–92
Emanuel, Hywel D. 'Geoffrey of Monmouth's *Historia regum Britanniae*: A Second
Variant Version' *Medium Ævum*, 35 (1966) 103–10
Faral, Edmond *La légende arthurienne* 3 vols Bibliothèque de l'École des Hautes Études,
Sciences historiques et philologiques, 255–7 (Paris 1929)
Fisher, D.J.V. *The Anglo-Saxon Age, c. 400–1042* (London 1973)
Flint, Valerie I.J. 'The *Historia regum Britanniae* of Geoffrey of Monmouth: Parody
and Its Purpose. A Suggestion' *Speculum*, 54 (1979) 447–68
Galbraith, V.H. *Historical Research in Medieval England: The Creighton Lecture in
History, 1949* (London 1951)
Gallais, Pierre 'La *Variant Version* de l'*Historia regum Britanniae* et le *Brut* de Wace'
Romania, 87 (1966) 1–32
Gransden, Antonia *Historical Writing in England c. 550 to c. 1307* (London 1974)
Haahr, Joan Gluckauf 'The Concept of Kingship in William of Malmesbury's *Gesta
regum* and *Historia novella*' *Mediaeval Studies*, 38 (1976) 351–71
Hammer, Jacob 'Note on a Manuscript of Geoffrey of Monmouth's *Historia regum
Britanniae*' *Philological Quarterly*, 12 (1933) 225–34
Hanning, Robert W. *The Vision of History in Early Britain: From Gildas to Geoffrey of
Monmouth* (New York and London 1966)
Harrison, Kenneth 'Woden' *Famulus Christi: Essays in Commemoration of the Thir-
teenth Centenary of the Birth of the Venerable Bede* ed Gerald Bonner (London 1976)
351–6
Houck, Margaret *Sources of the 'Roman de Brut' of Wace* University of California
Publications in English, 5/2 (Berkeley and Los Angeles 1941)
Hunter Blair, Peter *An Introduction to Anglo-Saxon England* 2nd ed (Cambridge 1977)
Huws, Daniel and Roberts, Brynley F. 'Another Manuscript of the Variant Version of

the *Historia regum Britanniae' Bulletin Bibliographique de la Société Internationale Arthurienne*, 25 (1973) 147–52

Jackson, Kenneth *Language and History in Early Britain: A Chronological Survey of the Brittonic Languages 1st to 12th C. A.D.* (Edinburgh 1953)

— 'On the Vulgar Latin of Roman Britain' *Mediaeval Studies in Honor of Jeremiah Denis Matthias Ford* eds Urban T. Holmes, Jr. and Alex J. Denomy (Cambridge Mass. 1948) 83–103

Johnson, Stephen *The Roman Forts of the Saxon Shore* (London 1976)

Keeler, Laura *Geoffrey of Monmouth and the Late Latin Chroniclers, 1300–1500* University of California Publications in English, 17/1 (Berkeley and Los Angeles 1946)

Kendrick, T.D. *British Antiquity* (London 1950)

Kerlouégan, F. 'Le Latin du *De excidio Britanniae* de Gildas' *Christianity in Britain, 300–700: Papers presented to the Conference on Christianity in Roman and Sub-Roman Britain held at the University of Nottingham 17–20 April 1967* eds M.W. Barley and R.P.C. Hanson (Leicester 1968) 151–76.

Levison, Wilhelm 'Bischof Germanus von Auxerre und die Quellen zu seiner Geschichte' *Neues Archiv der Gesellschaft für ältere deutsche Geschichtskunde*, 29 (1904) 95–175

— 'A Combined Manuscript of Geoffrey of Monmouth and Henry of Huntingdon' *English Historical Review*, 58 (1943) 41–51

— *England and the Continent in the Eighth Century* (Oxford 1946)

Miller, Molly 'Bede's Use of Gildas' *English Historical Review*, 90 (1975) 241–61

— 'The Last British Entry in the "Gallic Chronicles" ' *Britannia*, 9 (1978) 315–18

— 'Starting to Write History: Gildas, Bede and Nennius' *Welsh History Review*, 8 (1976–7) 456–65

Myres, J.N.L. *Anglo-Saxon Pottery and the Settlement of England* (Oxford 1969)

Nash, Daphne 'Reconstructing Poseidonios' Celtic Ethnography: Some Considerations' *Britannia*, 7 (1976) 111–26

O'Sullivan, Thomas D. *The 'De excidio' of Gildas: Its Authenticity and Date* Columbia Studies in the Classical Tradition, 7 (Leiden 1978)

Pähler, Heinrich *Strukturuntersuchungen zur 'Historia regum Britanniae' des Geoffrey of Monmouth* (Bonn 1958)

Parry, John J. 'The Chronology of Geoffrey of Monmouth's *Historia*, Books I and II' *Speculum*, 4 (1929) 316–22

Partner, Nancy F. *Serious Entertainments: The Writing of History in Twelfth-Century England* (Chicago and London 1977)

Plinval, G. de 'Les campagnes de saint Germain en Grande-Bretagne contre les Pélagiens' *Saint Germain d'Auxerre et son temps* (Auxerre 1950) 135–49

Saltmann, Avrom *Theobald, Archbishop of Canterbury* University of London Historical Studies, 2 (London 1956)

Schirmer, Walter F. *Die frühen Darstellungen des Arthurstoffes* Arbeitsgemeinschaft für Forschung des Landes Nordrhein-Westfalen, Geisteswissenschaften, 73 (Cologne and Opladen 1958)

Sisam, Kenneth 'Anglo-Saxon Royal Genealogies' *Proceedings of the British Academy*, 39 (1953) 287–348

Southern, R.W. 'Aspects of the European Tradition of Historical Writing, 1. The Classical Tradition from Einhard to Geoffrey of Monmouth' *Transactions of the Royal Historical Society*, 5th series, 20 (1970) 173–96

Spiegel, Gabrielle M. 'The Cult of Saint Denis and Capetian Kingship' *Journal of Medieval History*, 1 (1975) 43–69

Stenton, F.M. *Anglo-Saxon England* 3rd ed (Oxford 1971)

Stevens, C.E. 'Gildas Sapiens' *English Historical Review*, 56 (1941) 353–73

Stevenson, W.H. 'A Contemporary Description of the Domesday Survey' *English Historical Review*, 22 (1907) 72–84

Tatlock, J.S.P. *The Legendary History of Britain: Geoffrey of Monmouth's 'Historia regum Britanniae' and its Early Vernacular Versions* (Berkeley and Los Angeles 1950)

Thompson, E.A. 'Zosimus on the End of Roman Britain' *Antiquity*, 30 (1956) 163–7

Thomson, J. Oliver *History of Ancient Geography* (New York 1965)

Tierney, J.J. 'The Celtic Ethnography of Posidonius' *Proceedings of the Royal Irish Academy*, 60, series c (1959–60) 189–275

White, Donald A. *Litus Saxonicum: The British Saxon Shore in Scholarship and History* (Madison 1961)

Williamson, Dorothy M. 'Ralf son of Gilbert and Ralf son of Ralf' *Lincolnshire Architectural Society Reports and Papers*, NS 5 (1953) 19–27.

index

This book
was designed by
WILLIAM RUETER
and was printed by
University of
Toronto
Press